Applying Servant Leadership in Today's Schools

Mary K. Culver

Routledge
Taylor & Francis Group
New York London

First Published 2008 by Eye On Education

Published 2013 by Routledge
711 Third Avenue, New York, NY, 10017, USA
2 Park Square, Milton Park, Abingdon, Oxon OX14 4RN

Routledge is an imprint of the Taylor & Francis Group, an informa business

Library of Congress Cataloging-in-Publication Data

Culver, Mary K.
Applying servant leadership in today's schools / Mary K. Culver.
    p.cm.
  ISBN 978-1-59667-095-2
  1 . School management teams. 2. Leadership. I. Title.
LB2806.3.C85 2008
371.2-dc22
                                                    2008028496

ISBN 978-1-59667-095-2 (pbk)

Also Available from EYE ON EDUCATION

School Leader Internship:
Developing, Monitoring, and Evaluating
Your Leadership Experience, Second Edition
Martin, Wright, Danzig, Flanary, and Brown

Money and Schools, Fourth Edition
David C. Thompson, R. Craig Wood, and Faith E Crampton

Human Resources Administration:
A School-Based Perspective, Fourth Edition
Richard E. Smith

Introduction to Educational Administration:
Standards, Theories and Practice
Douglas J. Fiore

Transforming School Leadership with ISLLC and ELCC
Neil J. Shipman, J. Allen Queen, and Henry A. Peel

School-Community Relations, Second Edition
Douglas J. Fiore

Instructional Supervision:
Applying Tools and Concepts, Second Edition
Sally J. Zepeda

Introduction to Educational Leadership
and Organizational Behavior, Second Edition
Patti L. Chance

The Principal as Instructional Leader:
A Handbook for Supervisors, Second Edition
Sally J. Zepeda

The Administrator's Guide
to School Community Relations, Second Edition
George E. Pawlas

Countdown to the Principalship:
A Resource Guide for Beginning Principals
O'Rourke, Provenzano, Bellamy, and Ballek

What Great Principals Do Differently:
15 Things That Matter Most
Todd Whitaker

Table of Contents

1 Why We Can't Lead Alone **1**
Tips on Using This Book 7

2 Good-Bye to King of the Hill **9**
An Honest Look in the Mirror 11
Discussion 15
Self-Assessment 17
Admitting You Don't Know It All (And Yet, the World Still Turns) 17
Discussion 21
Self-Assessment 22
Become the "Principal" Learner: Seek the Answers 22
Discussion 26
Self-Assessment 27
Seek the Problems: Becoming the "Principal" Resource 28
Discussion 32
Self-Assessment 33

3 Learning to Play Nice **37**
Teacher Leadership Needed to Provide Stability 39
Discussion 43
Self-Assessment 45
New Agreements 45
Discussion 49
Self-Assessment 51
Equitable Resources 51
Discussion 55
Self-Assessment 56
Shared Accountability 56
Discussion 60
Self-Assessment 61

4 It's a Team Thing **65**
Professional Development 67
Discussion 71
Self-Assessment 72
Leading with the Teachers 72
Discussion 77
Self-Assessment 78
School Safety 78
Discussion 81
Self-Assessment 82
Special Programs 83

Discussion 86
Self-Assessment 86

5 The Whole Kit and Caboodle. 91
Addressing Cultural Awareness 93
Discussion 97
Self-Assessment 99
Promoting Parent Involvement 100
Discussion 104
Self-Assessment 105
Promoting Community Participation 106
Discussion 110
Self-Assessment 112
Working with the Central Office 112
Discussion 116
Self-Assessment 117

6 Follow the Leader. 121

References 133

Why We
Can't Lead Alone

As I walk my dog through the high desert each morning, I realize that I am his pack leader and notice that although he is faster than I am, I am leading the walk. He runs along, trying to sniff out his trail, while all along checking over his shoulder to see which direction I have chosen. Could he be mistaken for leading just because he is in front? Not if you measure leadership by moving people toward a common goal. The dog trusts me to make his walk interesting while allowing him to be a dog. I don't try to be a dog along with him; I don't have to, he recognizes me as his leader and wants to move in my direction.

This made me think about the concept of "leadership from behind." Why is it that we expect the leader to be in front of the followers? Because of definition? This defines a "leader" only in conventional terms. When we examine the true essence of leadership, we see that the best leadership comes from removing obstacles to the group from reaching its desired goal. Again, a lesson observed while walking the dog through the desert illustrates this. If you observe a group of people moving gingerly through the prickly desert foliage, you will notice that the leader might bravely bushwhack the trail, yet the followers hang back, cautious of following too close. Why? If you've ever had a thorny branch snap back into place in your face as the leader pushes it aside, you will understand why. However, if the leader holds the branch and allows the followers to pass through safely, the group follows much more quickly, even though the leader is no longer in front of the group. Moving the group safely, efficiently, and together toward the right destination is more important than pretending the leader has to be the one in front.

This concept is far from new. Greenleaf introduced the term "servant leadership" nearly 40 years ago, although the idea was thousands of years old then. Why have authors such as Senge, Wheatley, Covey, McGee, Goleman, Bennis, Collins, and so many more, taken up the call for leaders to be servants first? The answer might not be in the newness of the concept, but rather the unusualness of its practice. Our Founding Father, George Washington, ceremonially surrendered his sword to Congress after defeating the British and securing the treaty to end the Revolutionary War. This act of giving up power was uncommon for the circumstances. In fact you'd have to search eons of history to find other examples of powerful military leaders holding complete control of their country freely giving up that power. Further distinguishing his exemplary service, General Washington, himself, swung a pick to dig the trenches necessary to defeat Cornwallis at Yorktown. There was no shame in working alongside his troops, but rather a badge of honor to be found in his leadership example. Washington's loyalty was not to his own prestige, and not even to his army. His loyalty was to his country and the ideals of freedom it promised to so many. His leadership was that of a servant to his country, yet he is truly revered as one of the greatest leaders of history.

Just as with George Washington, it is not in our desire to make a name for ourselves that makes us great. It is the good we do for our organization that will make a lasting impact. The volumes of literature that have flooded the market for several decades continues to shine a light on the higher nature of leadership, however all too often, those in leadership positions take on the role of dictators. Do they set out to do so, or do the burdens of leadership and hassles of management grind down their noble ideals into a quick and dirty "get-it-done" attitude? The truth might be both. This work will give you strategies that will develop and maintain your pure ideals throughout your leadership tenure. We will explore what it means to "lead from behind" and the necessity of accepting a humble approach to leading a school.

Buzz words such as "servant leadership" become so widespread in leadership that we might become immune to the power behind the thought that went into making them so common. Before diving into the application of this book, a brief review of the elements of servant leadership is appropriate, as it is the essence of leading from behind.

Robert Greenleaf marked the difference between "servant-first" and "leader-first" leaders in his 1970 essay, *The Servant as Leader*. The "servant-first" leader seeks to ensure the needs of others are met, whereas the "leader-first" leader strives for personal power and possessions. Greenleaf clarifies elements of servant leadership in his revised *The Servant as Leader* (1991) book as listening, empathy, healing (of self and others), awareness (of others, situations, and self), persuasion, conceptualization, foresight, stewardship, commitment to growth of others, and building community (pp. 9–20). These behaviors create the practice of principled leadership, the kind of leadership capable of transcending human misery by enabling creativity to blossom.

The concepts of flattened hierarchies and shared leadership might frighten those leader-first leaders but fascinate those who enter leadership with a burning desire to serve. Max De Pree (1989) describes his ideal management process, participative management, as a belief in the potential of people. "Participative management guarantees that decisions will not be arbitrary, secret, or closed to questioning. Participative management is not democratic. Having a say differs from having a vote" (p. 25). He further elaborates that participation is "the opportunity and responsibility to have a say in your job, to have influence over the management of organizational resources based on your own competence and your willingness to accept problem ownership. No one person is the 'expert' at everything" (p. 48). Jim Collins (2001) echoes this point in his description of "Level 5" leaders who are "a study in duality: modest and willful, humble and fearless" (p. 22). He consistently found that leaders capable of taking their organizations "from good to great" directed their self-worth away from their own egos and focused their aspirations toward the success of their companies (p. 21). A "Level 4" leader might have the glitz to be a great personality, but producing a great program requires the dedicated humility of a "Level 5" leader (p. 27).

It is possible to practice leadership with very little experience or training, however, it develops through maturation. If maturation in a skill were not necessary, the genius Mozart would have written *The Marriage of Figaro* at age 12 instead of 30. The cycle of study, application, and self-reflection results in continual refinement of a skill; armchair quarterbacking is also an effective application for this process. This is why we analyze others' attempts to lead, and build our leadership plans from their mistakes and victories.

The goal of this book is to help you develop conviction in the ideal of servant leadership through careful illustration of how it applies specifically to school administration. Scenarios of real life school administrators will become your practice ground for analyzing their behaviors for elements of servant leadership. That analysis, in turn, will become the foundation of your own action plan for continual development as the caring, sharing, serving leader you want to be.

This book is designed around four major levels of personal development: intrapersonal, interpersonal, intra-organizational, and interorganizational. The first stage of developing as a true leader is the intrapersonal level. This is the level where we learn to accept ourselves as we are, without any pretense or fear. This level of leadership development focuses on understanding ourselves and our own capacities and limitations. Too often, new leaders step into the role assuming they must know everything, or at least appear to do so. This creates a smoke screen that fools very few besides the actor, but successfully stymies further growth. Growth is rarely possible if a need for it is not perceived, therefore, a habit of continual reflection is necessary. This level is addressed in Chapter 2, Good-Bye to the King of the Hill, using school leadership vignettes to illustrate the necessity and desirability of shared leadership.

After we come to recognize and accept our relationship with ourselves, we can freely begin to truly develop relationships with others. This is the interpersonal level of personal development necessary in becoming a servant leader. The interpersonal relationships stage of leadership development builds naturally out of the first. Once an inner acceptance of personal limitations is acknowledged, the need for building supportive, trusting relationships with others can be examined. Developing trust is the cornerstone to effective leadership. It has become the mantra of modern leadership, but it is so often overlooked in the daily grind of management. Again, day-to-day schoolhouse events are used in Chapter 3, Learning to Play Nice, to demonstrate the development of interpersonal relationships necessary to build this critical element. Various meanings of "shared" leadership will be analyzed through scenarios that address what participative leadership can mean in a school setting.

As important as teamwork is to modern leadership, it is possible only after a leader develops accepting and respectful relationships within themselves and with those around them. The intra-organizational relationship is that of a team, working together through a group of individuals striving for the same goal. At this level, we see maturation of shared leadership. Respect for our own leadership abilities combine with the trusting relationships we've built with members of our organization. This creates trusting relationships *among* groups within the organization. Serving as the leader, we capitalize on our awareness of strengths and weaknesses within ourselves and others, through coordinating collaboration in our organization. In Chapter 4, It's a Team Thing, we will analyze scenarios that illustrate how servant leadership could be used to maximize the potential of a school's faculty and staff.

When we come to grips with our own capacities, nurture relationships with all members of our organization, and empower them to work as teams, we are ready for the next step. Now, we can be truly successful in developing relationships between our organization and those outside of our domain. Cooperation, collaboration, and balance between our organization and others are created with the same calm and assertive leadership that fostered this within our organization. This interorganizational level of leadership development uses the same skills that created strong, supportive, and trusting networks in our organization, except now we are interacting with a greater community of participants.

Parent involvement, cultural sensitivity, and district politics are just a few of the interorganizational relationships that greatly suffer when the first three levels are not in good shape. How can your school operate effectively in your community if doubt and mistrust color relationships within your school? Yet, when the school functions in harmony within itself, it stands ready to build effective interactions outside of itself. In Chapter 5, Kit and Caboodle, we will reflect on how others have developed interorganizational relationships.

Chapter 6, Follow the Leader, asks the question: "Who *is* the leader we should follow?". Just as in the child's game by the same name, that role changes, adding creativity and excitement to the game. In school leadership, we must understand when a self-directed system works best, and when it impedes the smooth operation of a school. Examples of both cases will be presented, with a special caution not to slip down the "dark side" of autocratic leadership once success has been experienced by using limited doses of that style.

Tips on Using This Book

This book is designed to emphasize reflection on the practice of others and actively compare that to your own leadership practice. If you want to flip through the book and read scenarios out of order, go for it. Each was selected to stimulate your curiosity and interest in applying concepts of servant leadership to the realities of running a school. For best developmental results, however, I suggest that you work through each level of leadership in order. The sequence of the book moves you through the analysis, reflection, and planning stages inherent in the maturation process, one level of relationship building at a time.

Each chapter is divided into sections based on key issues facing school leaders. These sections consist of three true-life scenarios that represent various levels of applied servant leadership. In fact, many examples demonstrate just the opposite approach to leadership. Reflection questions prior to each scenario provide a cognitive set to help you analyze each, which is done by completing a chart at the end of each set of scenarios. Often, when reflecting on the actions of others, we think to ourselves, "I would never do that," or "That's a great idea," but we need to go further to make a viable plan to avoid or embrace the observed behavior. Each analysis chart has an area for you to jot down those ideas as they occur to you, so you can refer to them later in building an action plan. Following each analysis table, we will discuss what lessons in servant leadership we can draw from each set of scenarios.

At the end of each chapter you will reflect on your servant-leadership behaviors, and create a plan to polish and mature them. It is best if you actually write out your responses to each reflection question. This gives you a record of your progress, which might be used as part of your continual improvement process. Each chapter also provides you the opportunity to pull together an action plan to apply more servant leadership to your behavior. Finally, you will create a personalized assessment program to measure your progress on all your action plans developed in each chapter. This provides you, the reader, with a highly personal professional development plan for continually improving your application of servant leadership. No one will say this is easy; only that it is worth it, to you, and to your world.

Good-Bye to King of the Hill

The first level of development as a true servant leader occurs within the leader. A personal reflection of our abilities is necessary to accept the limitations to the term "leader." To free ourselves from the abuse of power wielding, we must recognize that one person will never possess all the information necessary to make the best decisions, nor have all the skills necessary to run an organization by himself or herself. This realization is actually the root of our true power as a leader. It allows us to willingly seek input and collaboration with other stakeholders. Furthermore, we strengthen both the quality of our decisions and the buy-in of those who will carry out those decisions by seeking input. Acknowledging our personal limitations is probably the single most important step toward creating a safe, enjoyable, effective environment for collaborative leadership.

An Honest Look in the Mirror

Scenario 1

As you read this passage, focus on the following questions:

- *Why does success at one level of leadership not necessarily predict success at another level?*
- *How did the principal's prior success inhibit her current performance?*
- *Was the principal's "burnout" as evident to her as it was to her former colleagues?*

"Wow, I can't believe that's the same Tracy." "I know, it's like the new job just ate her alive," two assistant principals (APs) whispered about their former colleague as they exited the restroom at a district administration meeting. Tracy, one of the brightest, best organized, and energetic APs in the district, had been promoted to principal at the same school only six months earlier. Everyone who knew her expected that she would be a tremendous success in the role; they were shocked at her rapid decline into physical and mental exhaustion. Her relationship with her husband and children suffered, as did that with members of her school. "It's just so hard, getting everything done," she told the APs in their restroom discussion. "It's like doing everything we used to do, plus all the duties of the other AP positions, and handling every little complaint or issue that the entire community has."

Scenario 2

As you read this passage, focus on the following questions:

- *What element is missing from this successfully fulfilled vision?*
- *What is the role of a leader in creating a long-lasting program?*
- *Does a successful leader guarantee continued organizational success?*

"We miss you; we really want you to come back," the board member told the former principal at a leadership convention. "No one has been able to run those schools like you did." "That doesn't surprise me," thought the former principal as she politely thanked the board member, "I did the work of four people in that position!" When the superintendent of her former accommodation school district first approached her to build a unified school out of the disjointed, ignored satellite programs, she had been honored at the chance to bring the benefits and accountability of an organized educational program to the dozen or so independent classrooms dotting the county district. She worked exhaustingly long hours in building a solid, supportive educational program. The previously unaccountable faculty and staff members had to be united into a collaborative team, cooperatively build a curriculum for the program, adopt a set of texts to be rotated through the sites, and justify the huge expense to the district. A regular supervision and professional development plan was implemented. When she left the district at the end of that exhaustingly successful year, the principal had handed over the entire blueprint for administering the program; a "yellow brick road" that no one else wanted to travel. A rapid succession of administrators tried, but failed to hold the program together. Although being flattered by the board member's comments, the principal couldn't help feeling like a failure. She had worked so hard to develop a lasting program but had succeeded only in being an outstanding employee.

Scenario 3

As you read this passage, focus on the following questions:

- *When does the need to increase teamwork override the need to practice delegation?*

- *What element was missing in the AP's point of reference regarding his investigation?*
- *To what degree did the principal's intervention in the investigation undermine the AP's authority? Support it? Demonstrate teamwork?*

"So, how is that mystery issue coming along for you," the principal asked his AP, walking through his office door. At the homecoming assembly earlier in the day, the AP had mentioned he was working on an important discipline issue, justifying his return to the office. "I'm still investigating, so I'd prefer to put off bothering you about it until I know more for sure." Trying to practice the fine art of delegation without micromanagement, the principal okayed the plan with a request for the AP to check in with him later. The morning dragged by without any word; following a hunch, the principal confronted the AP. "I'm following up on some leads, interviewing students, but still don't have the full story," the AP responded. Just then, a student walked into the office and blurted out, "Mr. B., Tony told me his friend from Phoenix is bringing a carload of his buddies over tonight to shoot up the dance." Putting the fear of micromanagement aside, the principal said, "I need to know what's going on here." His AP described a gang-related incident in the neighborhood the previous night involving some of the school's students, including a rumor of continuing the violence at the homecoming dance. Deciding to rally the troops, the principal called an emergency administrative team meeting. Each member, the dean, the athletic director, the AP, and the principal discussed the data at hand. Calling the chief of police to confirm the information, the administrative team and the police collectively decided the best move was to cancel the dance. Each team member jumped on their respective tasks to notify the school and community as smoothly as possible, pulling off the impossible before the 2:15 release bell.

Figure 2.1. Analysis Table 1

Directions: for each of the preceding scenarios, circle the leaders' level of self-awareness with an "L" (low), "M" (medium), or "H" (high) in the appropriate column. If helpful, note any evidence for your rating. Repeat this process to rate the leaders' ability to ask for help and the overall outcome of the situation. Finally, make note of any thoughts that you can apply to your own leadership in the Notes column. You should use these later to build your action plan.

	Level of Self-Awareness	Ability to Ask for Help	Overall Outcome
Scenario 1	L M H Evidence:	L M H Evidence:	L M H Evidence:
Notes:			
Scenario 2	L M H Evidence:	L M H Evidence:	L M H Evidence:
Notes:			
Scenario 3	L M H Evidence:	L M H Evidence:	L M H Evidence:
Notes:			

Discussion

There is a saying that individuals will rise to the level of their incompetence. That saying always bothered me. Why would a career on the rise end with incompetence? Although I still don't agree with it in many cases, I now know that competent people get promoted, but incompetent people do not. Therefore, people are promoted until they reach the level that they are no longer competent enough to rise above. You can see why I would have grounds to be bothered by this, and yet, when we examine the case of the principal in Scenario 1, we see a successful individual suddenly hit roadblocks to her success.

Prior success leads to promotions, but we cannot expect continued success in a new position if we do not adapt ourselves to our new situation. The principal in this first scenario tried to maintain the same level of involvement she had in her AP position. Furthermore, sensing that she should oversee all other aspects of the school, she took on direct involvement in the work of all her APs. On top of this, add the actual duties of a principal and it's no surprise that she had set herself up for exhaustion. Her "hard work" ethic failed her just as she reached her ideal level of leadership. Because she could not share responsibility and accountability with others, she took on an impossible workload and failed for the first time in her career. Even as her career, family life, and health crumbled around her, this individual could not recognize what she was doing was not what was needed. She applied the same work patterns, times 20, that had been successful at lower levels of leadership, and the more that failed, the more effort she applied. It never occurred to her that the answer to her problems lay in allowing others to share leadership. Rather than leading her team, she had insisted on giving them all "piggyback rides." Had she taken on, what was to her, the lesser role of supporting and inspiring the work of those around her, she might have found success, personally and as a leader.

According to Stephen Covey (Covey, Merrill & Merrill, 1994, p. 45), four inert desires of humanity are to live, to love, to learn, and to leave a legacy. It is probably the hope of leaving a legacy that drives many leaders to accept challenges others choose to ignore. As with the principal in Scenario 2, it is quite possible to be a highly successful leader without a long-lasting impact. Building a well-supported educational program was this leader's goal, and she met it. The training, resources, supervision, and collaborative spirit established were all very good things, yet they lacked the ability to sustain themselves. Is it possible that none of the leaders hired to carry on this program cared enough, were competent enough, or able to exert the charismatic control of factors to maintain the program? More likely, it was the core structure of the program. It had been designed and implemented by the will of one person. The only collaboration was confined to academic assignments. Actual control of the structure and maintenance of the program was never shared with those staff members who would remain the "constants" in the program.

In this case, a lasting legacy would have been a program that could sustain itself through the leadership inherent in the staff, rather than the memory of a "great leader" who could not be replaced. The vision of a leader can be shared with others to produce wonderful outcomes, but unless the vision is that of the staff, it is unlikely to outlive the tenure of the leader. When one has established leadership throughout his or her organization, whether or not he or she is identified with that change over the years, that individual has created the most meaningful legacy a leader can have.

If we want to create an organization that allows leadership to flourish at every level, how do we handle a situation where someone desperately wants to lead alone? When we hold the belief that the essence of leadership is to serve others so they can perform better and achieve more, the answer becomes evident. The art of delegation is so difficult to master for many would-be leaders, as they struggle to stop doing all the work in exchange for enabling others to do it more efficiently. Fearing the trap of micromanagement, many good-hearted leaders leave others to their tasks, regardless of their preparedness. Knowing when to provide guidance and direction is vital to effective servant leadership, just as knowing when to set limits and boundaries for children is important to parenting. We recognize that parents must instruct and steer children in life while preparing them to stand on their own as functional adults. We worry, however, that doing the same for developing leaders will lead to the dreaded micromanagement. Ironically, when our purpose is to develop shared leadership capacity, the right course of action can be micromanagement, as long as that means redistributing authority to increase teamwork.

The AP in Scenario 3 was working to do his duty to the best of his ability. The principal had established a zone of trust in providing the freedom to conduct his investigation as he saw fit *and* by requesting feedback on the situation. When the feedback did not come within a "reasonable" amount of time, that zone became violated in the sense that the absence of free-flowing information limits the spirit of teamwork. In his desire to handle a volatile situation by himself, the AP forgot the key to shared leadership is "sharing." By opening the door to communication on the issue, the principal placed a limitation on the AP's control of the investigation, but at the same time, he supported it by placing him in the center of the team's investigation. Just as important as preventing the violence planned for that evening, the principal needed to demonstrate the process of sharing leadership. Clearly, this administrative team did not yet function as a team, and by placing some skill-appropriate limitations on the exercise of authority, the principal modeled the process of team problem-solving. As important as that lesson was, it was secondary to the need of capitalizing on the skills of all team members to safely resolve the issue within the short time available.

Self-Assessment

- Do you approach your current job with the same tactics you used in previous positions?
- Have you "promoted" yourself in your mind? (Do you embrace a new set of duties?)
- Do you monitor subtle changes in your health or family and social lives?
- Would the changes you've implemented continue to flourish if you left your position today? (Have you built a lasting system of shared leadership?)
- Do you teach, and model, teamwork and shared leadership at every opportunity?
- Do you build ability and trust among your team?
- Are you able to delegate responsibilities at skill-appropriate levels?
- How do you assess and monitor team members' skill?

Admitting You Don't Know It All
(And Yet, the World Still Turns)

Scenario 4

As you read this passage, focus on the following questions:
- *Prior to the staff survey, had the principal known he had weaknesses?*
- *Did he believe that he had sufficiently hidden those weaknesses from his followers?*
- *Would the legitimacy of his leadership be strengthened or weakened by admitting he was still developing? Why?*

The principal figuratively shook in his shoes as he stood in front of his staff, presenting their collective feedback on his leadership behavior. A week prior, he had collected anonymous surveys from the entire staff, rating his leadership. After analyzing the feedback, he prepared his personal professional development plan, as well as the presentation he was making to the staff. "If I want 'continual improvement' to be accepted as part of our vision, I have to model it," he justified. Pointing out the highs, and lows, of his performance based on the feedback, he presented his plan for developing the areas indicating need. For the most part, the staff had seen through the "imposter" and knew exactly what his strengths and weaknesses were. "Funny," he thought, "they still treated me like I was the principal, anyway."

Scenario 5

As you read this passage, focus on the following questions:

- *What is it about an emergency situation that causes people to crave strong leadership?*
- *Did the principal's actions seem to provide comforting leadership to her community?*
- *How do the principal's thoughts reveal her hidden doubts about her role?*

The date was September 11, 2001, a bit over two years since the principal had been hired at the school. Watching the television as the second plane crashed into the Towers, she knew she had to get to her school as quickly as possible. Intuitively, she knew people would want her presence, and yet, all she wanted to do was call her mother for reassurance. Arriving on campus long before the first busses, she was sought out by the head of security, looking for direction on what to do. Teachers huddled in groups in the administration office, seeking comfort, and office staff was wide-eyed with fright. The phones began ringing with concerned parents on the lines, asking if school was canceled and would their children be safe. The principal was the first to answer a call, assuring the parent that the school was braced for high alert, would be in full lock down, that its semi-rural setting wasn't likely to be the next Al Qaeda target, and of course she could keep her child at home if she felt she should. The office staff followed her lead, as a similar message was sent to all faculty and staff through an announcement for them to check their e-mail for the emergency procedure to follow. Administration and security spent the day escorting students to the restrooms, checking in on teachers (especially those with ties to New York), and playing the role of guardian and protector to the entire school community. One usually tough, swaggering student asked the principal as she walked him to the restroom, "Are we going to die, Miss?" "No, son, we aren't," she assured him. She could see that he calmed at her assurance and wondered, secretly, if he would relax in the same manner if he only knew those comforting words came from a scared little girl deep inside the principal.

Scenario 6

As you read this passage, focus on the following questions:

- *What are some reasons to support the AP's preconceived idea on student placement in the honor's program?*
- *Is there any indication that the AP had doubts about his instructional leadership capacity?*
- *To what degree does the AP's confidence in his opinion obstruct exploration of appropriate compromise?*

"It's always this department," the AP thought with disgust. "Why are they such student haters?" He was trying to resolve an issue brought to the school's curriculum leadership committee by the English department. "Admissions to the Honor's Program" was the benign way of issuing a challenge to the administrative decision to allow all students who asked for placement in "honor's" classes to be admitted. The faculty felt there should be more considerations made prior to placement to maintain the integrity of the honor's program. "I'm the head of instruction on this campus. Why won't they just accept that all students have the right to be in an honor's class?," the AP asked the committee. Several faculty members just looked down at the table, resigned that this administrator would not be any assistance in developing a fair and acceptable admittance procedure. They had already presented him with research and data on the subject, and it didn't even cause a moment of reflection on his position.

Figure 2.2. Analysis Table 2

Directions: For each of the preceding scenarios, circle the leaders' level of self-awareness with an "L" (low), "M" (medium), or "H" (high) in the appropriate column. If helpful, note any evidence for your rating. Repeat this process to rate the leaders' ability to ask for help and the overall outcome of the situation. Finally, make note of any thoughts that you might apply to your own leadership in the Notes column. You should use these later to build your action plan.

	Level of Self-Awareness	Ability to Ask for Help	Overall Outcome
Scenario 4	L M H Evidence:	L M H Evidence:	L M H Evidence:
Notes:			
Scenario 5	L M H Evidence:	L M H Evidence:	L M H Evidence:
Notes:			
Scenario 6	L M H Evidence:	L M H Evidence:	L M H Evidence:
Notes:			

Discussion

Despite our best efforts to project the image of an ideal leader, the fact remains that we are only human, and that is not a sad fact. Being human makes you one of the group, a coconspirator in the game of life. Being a leader puts you in the position to influence the outcomes of that game. When you take a good look in the mirror, you can be frank with what you see, lumps, bumps, and all. Of course, it's natural to smooth these over and try to cover the flaws before going out in public, presenting a more polished view of ourselves. This presentation is expected, but it doesn't really change what is underneath. Taking stock in what you have, making a plan to improve that, and holding yourself accountable to that plan is the only lasting way to "smooth our lumps." Surprisingly, on the professional front, too many would-be leaders feel they need to cram themselves into "administrative spandex" to present an image of artificial perfection. It is as it they expect rejection if they do not convey the ideal leadership appearance. Unfortunately, this behavior does not allow for actually improving one's skills in leadership. It diverts our energy from actually serving our followers to trying to maintain the "imposter." In the end, the only one that is fooled by the pretence is our would-be leader. Followers understand lumps and bumps, as they have their own. Certainly, followers appreciate competence and confidence in their leaders, but above all, they value honesty. By stripping off the mask of perfection and humbly asking their followers to participate in their professional development, a leader models self reflection, continual improvement, and a desire to be an effective leader.

There are few times when a top-down, authoritarian style of leadership is not only acceptable, but desired. When the building is on fire, our desire to form a committee and come to consensus on how to evacuate is greatly diminished. We want someone to take charge and get us safely out of danger. In a crisis situation, people crave strong leadership, and that includes the leaders. It has been said by countless heroes that fear and bravery go hand in hand. Without knowing there is danger, no action can truly be considered heroic, it would simply be routine. It is in knowing the danger, but taking the action anyway, that an action becomes bravery. By recognizing one's limitations, but taking the required actions to be the leader others need, one quells the doubt of "can I do this?" This is truly servant leadership, as one ignores fear, and even without "all the answers," steps in to provide the leadership behavior necessary under the conditions. No one except the principal in Scenario 5 questioned her qualifications to comfort the school community. It was her behaviors, not her resume that led that community that day.

Assuming we have all the knowledge and skills necessary to lead any given situation might be just as common as secretly doubting our right to lead. Perhaps, it is even more of a handicap to effective leadership, as these individuals are not even aware that they don't know everything. In other words, they are blinded by their own imposter. There are many reasons why people begin to believe their own press about their abilities: intensive study, lengthy experience, flattery and pandering taken to heart, or pure ego run amuck. This is when one's leadership is most ineffective. Sure, you might get your way, as power wielders do, but you are not leading. There will be no lasting influence of your actions once you are gone. When leaders become so convinced of their abilities that they feel no need for additional information before determining the course of action, they cripple collaboration, destroy innovation, and halt their own development as leaders. Is it any wonder that humility is a key factor in servant leadership? To move others in any direction, you must be mobile yourself.

Self-Assessment

- Are you generally aware of what you do not know?
- Do you prefer making "command" decisions rather than "collaborative" ones on topics where you are an expert?
- Are you aware of the limitations of your knowledge and/or skills?
- Have you ever conducted a formal 360-degree leadership assessment?
- Did you make the results of that assessment and your corresponding professional development plan public?
- Do you set aside any personal doubts or fears during times of crisis to provide needed leadership behavior for others?
- What evidence do you have to indicate your leadership is beneficial to others, despite your human flaws?

Become the "Principal" Learner: Seek the Answers

Scenario 7

As you read this passage, focus on the following questions:

- *What is the importance of understanding one's limitations in leadership roles?*
- *When creating a work team from individuals, each lacking the ability to complete the task alone, what factors lead to success?*

- *In what ways did a humble, collaborative approach to instructional leadership produce better results than two years of authoritarian directives?*

"I don't care if it's the teachers' responsibility to write their curriculum," the principal told his AP. "He's had two years and hasn't produced a thing. I need you to get it done." To make matters more difficult, the curriculum in question was for the school's agriculture magnet program. "How am I going to write curriculum for this program?" the AP asked himself. "I can't even grow beans." He contacted the district's vocational education supervisor and met with her for several hours, reviewing everything from what was required from her end, to what had been used in the past. Next, he met with the agriculture teacher, who was reluctant to write the curriculum because of confusion about what a "curriculum" actually was. The teacher appeared knowledgeable of the content, state standards, and vocational program requirements, but lacked the skills necessary to knit that into a structured curriculum for the program. The AP arranged a meeting with the state director of vocational programs, and held a phone conference with a member of the Agricultural Education Board from a local university. After meeting with these resources, the AP and the agriculture teacher came to an understanding: The AP understood the curriculum process, and the teacher understood the content. Together, they slowly created the agriculture curriculum after school hours and during prep periods, with much support from district, state, and university personnel.

Scenario 8

As you read this passage, focus on the following questions:
- *Does "knowing" something always make it "so"?*
- *How could the principal have used all the experience in the room without looking as if he wasn't "in charge"?*
- *What is likely to happen to "informational resources" if they are never tapped?*

The school's administrative team sat around the conference table, building the school's emergency plan. The head of security, a retired police officer, joined them in this exercise. The topic of riot, terrorism, or other catastrophic occurrences was being discussed, along with proposed procedures for dealing with each. Repeatedly, the question of what call the principal should make, at what point, was addressed. The only female in the room, an AP new to the district, pointed out, "That decision is often the police department's to make, if they've declared the situation a police matter." The retired police officer nodded in agreement, while another AP shouted her down, "Not true; the principal is always in control of the school. It's always the principal's decision!" The principal concurred that he would always be the final decision-maker, regardless of the crisis. The first AP and the security chief exchanged defeated looks, and the process rolled on.

Scenario 9

As you read this passage, focus on the following questions:

- *Why was there no sense of "shame" in the lack of testing protocol for this administrator?*
- *How could time spent researching an effective plan be justified down the road?*
- *What was the connection between the "architect(s)" of the protocol and those who would implement it? Why is this important?*

Being a brand new high school, there was no set protocol for standardized testing. The AP had the responsibilities to assign students to proctors and rooms, in-service the proctors on test security and administration, distribute testing materials, and collect, sort, package, and return tests. He asked his administrative assistant to discuss the process with some of her counterparts at established schools, while he did the same. The counseling department was also consulted before a draft plan was drawn. This plan was sent out to the staff, and feedback was requested. Little came in, but all was considered. The final plan was distributed and implemented. Afterwards, the staff was surveyed for their opinions of what went well, and what needed to be adjusted. The AP met with his assistant, and they reviewed the feedback, creating a revised protocol for the next standardized test. This, too, was reported to the staff for their input. Over the years, the process continued to be refined, and often the only staff feedback was simply, "This was the smoothest testing procedure I've encountered. Thank you for your attention to this matter."

Figure 2.3. Analysis Table 3

Directions: For each of the preceding scenarios, circle the leaders' level of self-awareness with an "L" (low), "M" (medium), or "H" (high) in the appropriate column. If helpful, note any evidence for your rating. Repeat this process to rate the leaders' ability to ask for help and the overall outcome of the situation. Finally, make note of any thoughts that you might apply to your own leadership in the Notes column. You should use these later to build your action plan.

	Level of Self-Awareness	Ability to Ask for Help	Overrall Outcome
Scenario 7	L M H Evidence:	L M H Evidence:	L M H Evidence:
Notes:			
Scenario 8	L M H Evidence:	L M H Evidence:	L M H Evidence:
Notes:			
Scenario 9	L M H Evidence:	L M H Evidence:	L M H Evidence:
Notes:			

Discussion

If there is one theme I would hope you adopt from reading this book, it would be that there is no shame in needing others to help lead. In fact, there is a badge of honor for those who recognize that they are not the "end all" of knowledge, and that others have meaningful input to make. Rather than doom your organization to the level of one person's knowledge, open the gates of unlimited possibilities by tapping into everyone's knowledge. That is true leadership! Imagine two games: Follow the Leader and Red Rover. The team captain in Follow the Leader heads a line of followers, complacently trailing behind the leader. It's evident to anyone who's leading, but what gets done? How long is it "fun" to play this game? Conversely, in Red Rover, it is difficult to identify the team captain in the middle of play because all team members are actively engaged in the game's objective: maintaining a tight connection despite outward challenges hoping to tear the group apart. The successful leader in this game coordinates the efforts of all members, strategically organizing them to maximize the strength of each, so there is no "weak link." This game generates a much higher level of enthusiasm among participants than Follow the Leader, resulting in longer play. That is the model for leadership that will produce uncommon results and draw people to participate. If leaders insist on standing alone, they are the weakest link.

Just as in Red Rover, we are less likely to withstand, let alone overcome, challenges if we stand alone. In rallying the team to triumph over any foe and strategically organizing our team to maximize its strengths, we achieve what was not possible alone. By recognizing his own limitations in meeting the principal's demand to produce an agriculture curriculum, the AP in Scenario 7 could accept the agriculture teacher's limitations and focus instead on each of their strengths. Furthermore, rather than trying to hide his limitations, the AP exposed them to others in his request for assistance, at the district, state, and professional levels. Rather than shame, he achieved success—success in developing the required curriculum and success in leadership.

Contrary to his Scenario 7 counterpart, the AP in Scenario 8 takes the hard line of declaring his knowledge to be exact and unchallengeable, even though disputed. Had proper humility for the act of leadership been applied to that situation, the opposing point of view would have at least been fully heard, discussed, and perhaps investigated further. The principal failed in rushing to a hasty decision by emotionally connecting to the piece of advice that supported his point of view rather than hearing out differing opinions. If there is one certainty in life, it is that there is no certainty in life. Simply "knowing" something does not always mean that it is so. Was it worth the risk of handcuffs and arrest to insist that a principal would retain control of the campus during a police emergency? Would that be worth the image of "total confidence" portrayed in the leadership team meeting? When leaders reject information to maintain an illusion of "master and commander," they run the risk of eliminating that source of information. When input to a situation is blatantly rejected, participation shrinks. Even when contributions are politely disregarded, bypassed, or overturned, leaders doom themselves, and their organization, to the limits of their own certainty.

Too often, leaders assume they must be seen as unsurpassed in every aspect of the organization to command the respect of their subordinates. Although leaders can, and should, become knowledgeable of their organization, the truth is as you move up the ranks, your role moves from "specialist" toward "leader." Using an orchestra as an example, the leader is expected to "conduct." He or she is not expected to play principal violin, viola, trumpet, bassoon, and percussion! Although the conductor might have mastered one of these areas, music in general, and hold some training in each of the other specialty areas, his or her role is no longer to "play" the performance but to conduct it. There is no shame for the conductor if he or she is unable to teach an oboist a needed technique. The conductor's role is to recognize the need for the technique, bring it to the oboist's attention, and perhaps prescribe a course of action for the oboist to pursue. The same principle applies to school leaders. The expertise of your staff will outweigh your own, and this is a good thing. It does not make you less of an expert in your area, but it does mean your role has changed from "principal performer" to "conductor." Now is your chance to lead the collaboration of dozens of "experts." By placing the "instruments" in the hands of your "orchestra," you are free to interpret the score, and lead them to balance, harmony, and stellar performances. It is in accepting the need for each member of the team to contribute their unique talents to the overall effort that an individual becomes able to lead. Working with, and through, those who execute the necessary duties is the only way to achieve their very best performance. That is, unless you are a one-person orchestra.

Self-Assessment

- ◆ How often do you admit that you don't know something?
- ◆ How often do you say "I'll get back to you on that" and then research the topic before responding?
- ◆ Do you try to model life-long learning, curiosity, and a "we are smarter than me" attitude?
- ◆ Are you confident in your abilities even when working collaboratively with various levels of specialists?

- In what ways do you actively seek information during your day-to-day operations?
- Do you open lines of information by respectfully considering all input?
- How often do you seek feedback before implementing important decisions? Minor decisions?

Seek the Problems:
Becoming the "Principal" Resource

Scenario 10

As you read this passage, focus on the following questions:

- *To what degree is an administrator responsible for providing guidance to new employees?*
- *Is ignorance of the job a valid excuse for the teacher? For the administrators?*
- *How would the outcomes of this scenario be different if the principal had spent his time inducting the coach instead of "investigating" her?*

The principal shifted through a stack of papers, waiting for the first-year teacher and coach to respond to his summons. He had all his documentation in order: several days worth of investigation, student interviews, and a copy from the faculty handbook on student funds. Granted, the teacher in question was a true "newbie" and teaching six classes (four different preps), but as the cheerleading coach, she had violated school policy. For more than a week, candy fund-raiser flyers were circulating the school, yet no petition for a fund-raiser had been approved by the student council, and no funds had been deposited into the Cheerleading bookstore account. The teacher entered his office with her "deer in the headlights" look, carrying the items he had requested just five minutes earlier. It surprised him that she already had a detailed accounting of all the funds collected, as if she'd made her own deposit slip for the cash. Having confronted her with his knowledge that she was conducting a secret fundraiser, he brushed off her explanation that she was unaware of policy regulating student funds. She told him there was nothing in the handbook about student funds or fund-raising to guide her. "Aha!" he thought, as he pulled out the photocopy of page 127 of the handbook, "I have proof right here." The young teacher read the copied page in disbelief. There, listed under Teacher and Student Funds was the required procedure. Why hadn't she thought to look in the "T's" for fund-raising? Content that he'd caught a felon, the principal handed her a letter of reprimand to sign. Again, the teacher explained she had tried to find guidance in the matter. Softening a bit, the principal countered, "During my first three years in this job, I had an outstanding AP who dealt with training the coaches, and I relied on that. This is John's first year in the job, and he is still learning it. Now, if you'd just sign on that line, this will go to your personnel file for three years."

Scenario 11

As you read this passage, focus on the following questions:
- *Does status quo equal success?*
- *What good is asking for information if it is not acted on?*
- *What role did "positional authority" play in creating and/or removing an obstacle for employees?*

As she read through the weekly communication form comments, the AP paused to look outside her office door at the unused locking mailboxes across from her door. Why were they there? The mailroom on the other side of the administration building housed all the 9×12 inch mailboxes for faculty, administration, and staff, or so she had thought. According to the comment on the communication form in her hand, classified employees shared a single mailbox within their department, while the locking mailboxes went empty. A few minutes of research resulted in the history of the locking mailboxes: They had originally been installed for faculty, but grading forms would not fit inside without being bent. Therefore, the mailroom had been built, but there was not enough space for the more than 80 staff members to have large mailboxes, so they shared. A few more quick discussions led to distribution of mailbox keys to all staff members, giving each of them an individual, secure mailbox and providing meaningful purpose to a previously overlooked resource.

Scenario 12

As you read this passage, focus on the following questions:
- *What behaviors might have led to this problem going previously undiagnosed?*
- *Was the principal capable of resolving the issue alone?*
- *What does it mean to "be visible" on campus?*

Standing in her red silk skirt suit, beads of sweat ran down the newly appointed principal's face and disappeared under the neckline of her blouse as she listened to leaders of the football team explain their working conditions. "We've never seen a principal in the weight room, before," they told her. She could almost understand that, as the sweltering heat plastered her once pristine outfit to her body. "Isn't there any cooling in this room?" she asked. A collective groan was issued from the young men doing their morning workout. "They disconnected the swamp cooler when they started the renovations, Miss." This was a shocker. Not only was it July in Arizona, but school would be starting in August, and this building was scheduled to house the entire physical education program. The outgoing principal had told her the renovations were scheduled through November, and she was just beginning to realize nothing had been done to arrange cooling for the facility. A quick phone call to a local gym gave the football team a two-week pass to train in an air-conditioned facility. Several other phone calls led to a tour of the school gym by the school and district athletic directors, district business director, construction foreman, and campus maintenance chief. As they loosened their ties to accommodate the sweat rolling down their necks, the principal only smiled as they quickly came to an agreement to bring in a temporary air-conditioning unit for the gym.

Figure 2.4. Analysis Table 4

Directions: For each of the preceding scenarios, circle the leaders' level of self-awareness with an "L" (low), "M" (medium), or "H" (high) in the appropriate column. If helpful, note any evidence for your rating. Repeat this process to rate the leaders' ability to ask for help and the overall outcome of the situation. Finally, make note of any thoughts that you might apply to your own leadership in the Notes column. You should use these later to build your action plan.

	Level of Self-Awareness	Ability to Ask for Help	Overall Outcome
Scenario 10	L M H Evidence:	L M H Evidence:	L M H Evidence:
Notes:			
Scenario 11	L M H Evidence:	L M H Evidence:	L M H Evidence:
Notes:			
Scenario 12	L M H Evidence:	L M H Evidence:	L M H Evidence:
Notes:			

Discussion

There is a distinct learning curve whenever we move from one position to another. We become comfortable with what we know how to do, and when we leave that comfort zone, as we must if we are to progress, an adjustment period is necessary to build new comfort with our new surroundings. One of the easiest ways to make a transition into any new lifestyle is to have a guide, someone who is familiar with the territory and willing to help acclimatize the newcomer. This is why induction programs and mentoring are so popular for new teachers and new administrators. At what point, however, are we expected to stand on our own two feet?

In Scenario 10, we encounter two individuals in need of guidance. The first is a third-year administrator who had relied heavily on his previous assistant to provide needed training and supervision of personnel. The second is a first-year teacher with a near crippling load of teaching six classes, four different preps, and coaching cheerleading throughout the year. When the principal no longer had his guide, he found himself with both a new assistant and new teachers without adequate support in learning their new jobs. Had he shared his leadership duties, or abandoned them altogether? The answer can be found in the connection between shared leadership and servant leadership. We must never confuse sharing leadership with neglecting leadership. Although no one person is expected to know everything and be able to do everything, we must be able to work collectively to ensure that someone does. The leader's role is to see that everyone has access to whatever they need to gain the knowledge and skills necessary to do their jobs. That's the servant part of the leadership role.

A large part of being a servant leader is the active role one plays to seek out obstacles to success and remove them. Open communication is critical in this role, as status quo is the exact opposite of such growth. An attitude of genuine caring about the needs of the team must be established before the trust necessary for collaborative leadership emerges. Complaints generally are not the same as constructive contribution to the leadership effort for the organization, yet they are a beginning. When opportunity to voice concerns and ideas is received and acted on by leaders, followers begin to be transformed into team members. By having their opinions impact the organization, personnel see that they are taken seriously as contributing members of the organization. Complaints can be replaced with more productive suggestions, and the doorway to collaboration is opened. A wealth of information exists within the members of an organization, waiting for someone with positional authority to tap into it, and implement positive changes based on it.

Despite this, some administrators choose to base their decisions on the information they, or perhaps a small group of advisors, possess. Scenario 12 illustrates the downfall associated with that behavior. The outgoing administration of the school had carefully planned stages of reconstruction on the campus, using the information gleaned within office meetings. Unfortunately, they had never set foot in the facility in question under the conditions they proposed. Leaving the weight room without cooling during the hot Arizona summer and early fall was an unintended consequence of their rebuilding efforts. Management by walking around cannot become a mere catch phrase; nor can it be relegated to "snoopervision" of personnel. Regularly walking every aspect of the organization is critical to understanding working conditions that can hamper the capacity to produce positive results for personnel. This visibility of leaders is compounded when their tours combine with open conversations with the local stakeholders. As with our new principal in this scenario, walking the trenches might increase a leader's dry cleaning tab, but it will be worth it, and more, to identify and remove barriers to success. Collaboration in identifying issues is the first step in collaboration in improving those issues. No leader can afford to stand alone.

Self-Assessment

- Do you delegate your responsibilities, or neglect them?
- When you rely on the special skills of subordinates, are you learning from them, so that you could do what they do, or teach someone else to do it?
- Have you ever considered your own learning curve before criticizing that of others?
- In what way do you actively and regularly seek new information?
- How do you use that information?
- Do you share that information with others to properly respond to it?
- How do you provide feedback on other's input?
- Do you thank people for their input?

Figure 2.5. Action Plan 1

Having completed the analysis charts for all topics in this chapter, focus on your Notes column for each. Use your notes to complete this action plan (Figure 2.5) for applying these ideas to your own leadership style.

An Honest Look in the Mirror

Goal: (Describe the leadership characteristics you hope others see in you.)

_____

_____

_____

Assessment: (How and when will you measure your progress toward your goal?)

_____

_____

_____

Action Steps:

1._____

_____

_____

2. _____

_____

_____

3. _____

_____

_____

_____

Admitting You Don't Know It All
(and Yet, the World Still Turns)

Goal: (Describe how you will avoid allowing your personal limitations from restricting your leadership.)

_____

_____

_____

Assessment: (How and when will you measure your progress toward your goal?)

_____
_____
_____
_____

Action Steps:

1. _____
_____
_____

2. _____
_____
_____

3. _____
_____
_____

Become the "Principal" Learner:
Seek the Answers

Goal: (Describe what you will do to continually seek new information, knowledge, and skills.)

_____
_____
_____
_____

Assessment: (How and when will you measure your progress toward your goal?)

_____
_____
_____

Action Steps:

1. _____
_____
_____

2. _____
_____

3. _____

_____

_____

Seek the Problems:
Becoming the "Principal" Resource

Goal: (Describe the behaviors you will demonstrate to continually remove obstacles for your organization.)

_____

_____

_____

Assessment: (How and when will you measure your progress toward your goal?)

_____

_____

_____

Action Steps:

1. _____

_____

_____

2. _____

_____

_____

3. _____

_____

_____

Learning
to Play Nice

Interpersonal relationships can build naturally off inner-personal relationship development. Once inner acceptance of personal limitations is acknowledged, the need for building supportive and trusting relationships with others can unfold. Prior to building effective networks among sections of a school and with agencies outside of the organization leaders must be able to create trusting and healthy relationships with their staff members. Assuming the prior intrapersonal development, this chapter addresses turning one's leadership outward, to constituents of the school.

Teacher Leadership Needed to Provide Stability

Scenario 13

As you read this passage, focus on the following questions:

- *What possible reasons would cause a district to routinely shuffle school administrators around the district?*
- *How could this practice negatively impact the schools?*
- *What is the level of interpersonal trust demonstrated in this incident?*

It's the beginning of another 10 1/2–month contract year for the assistant principals (APs) in a large, inner-city high-school district. Across the district, administrators wait nervously by their fax machines. Following their philosophy of "keeping things fresh," the district officials regularly transfer administrators among its 10 schools; notifying the administrators through a facsimile was just the preferred method of making the change. Next to one AP, the familiar whirl and screech of the fax indicates that at least one member of the administrative team is about to be reassigned to another school. A cover page emerges, addressed to this assistant: "Dr. Smith, you have been assigned to," and there the machine died, leaving Dr. Smith hanging in anticipation. Calling the human resource office to determine where his new assignment was to be, he is told that information could not be given over the phone.

Scenario 14

As you read this passage, focus on the following questions:
- *Why did the principal target morale improvement over test improvement?*
- *In what ways were both goals intertwined?*
- *Were the principal's efforts in vain?*

The school is in its second year of failing to meet Adequate Yearly Progress (AYP), and morale among the faculty and staff is at an all time low. There has been a new principal every year for the last five school years. The last principal left the school in shambles, with missing records, no paper trail, and many empty promises. More than 50 percent of the faculty had resigned or transferred, the remaining staff is highly skeptical. The new principal officially begins her new position on July 1 and teachers report on July 11. Shortly after her hire date in late May, the superintendent gives her the directive to improve the school's climate and resolve the AYP problem. She sets about increasing staff morale as her primary goal, nurturing staff and returning an element of personal caring and fun to the school environment in every action. As she slowly gathers the trust of the faculty, she opens dialog among them on how to improve student learning and meet the adequate yearly progress benchmarks. Teacher committees and task forces tackled data analysis, researched school-based instructional practices, and identified specific improvement strategies. The teachers further committed to arranging in-service trainings and implementing peer-to-peer accountability in instructional practice. Morale and test scores increased, and teachers who had transferred were heard to regret their decision based on positive changes brought on by the new principal. Unfortunately, the scores did not increase sufficiently that first year to avoid the harsh state consequence of removing the principal from her position. Fortunately, her reforms created a permanent student-centered teacher leadership base that continued to improve student performance, and her reputation preceded her into her new principal position.

Scenario 15

As you read this passage, focus on the following questions:
- *Why would teachers sabotage teacher-leadership efforts?*

- *In what ways is effective school leadership similar to effective classroom leadership?*
- *How can leaders maintain enthusiasm for building teacher leadership in the face of opposition?*

Giving a heavy sigh, the principal lamented the "tall poppy" syndrome that stymied his efforts to increase teacher leadership at his school. It seemed the culture of the school discouraged teachers by quickly "cutting them down to size" whenever someone's head popped above the rest of the field. His assistant commented that perhaps he should approach the situation the same way he recently observed a teacher using in the classroom; proactively developing a supportive environment. Just as many teachers of the school seemed to excel individually in creating safe learning environments for their students, he could enlist the faculty in designing a safe professional environment, similar to those they create for students in their classrooms. Taking this parallel further, he also realized that his teachers ensured student success by teaching the specific skills students needed, therefore, he decided he must proactively teach teacher leadership skills such as facilitation, conflict resolution, data analysis and research. He smiled as he rolled up his sleeves and began drafting his "curriculum scope and sequence" and "lesson plans" for developing teacher leadership throughout his school.

Figure 3.1. Analysis Table 5

Directions: For each of the preceding scenarios, circle the level of trust between the leader and others with an "L" (low), "M" (medium), or "H" (high) in the appropriate column. If helpful, note any evidence for your rating. Repeat this process to rate the effectiveness of the working environment and the overall outcome of the situation. Finally, make note of any thoughts that you can apply to your own leadership in the Notes column. You should use these later to build your action plan.

	Trust between Leader and Others	Effectiveness of Working Environment	Overall Outcome
Scenario 13	L M H Evidence:	L M H Evidence:	L M H Evidence:
Notes:			
Scenario 14	L M H Evidence:	L M H Evidence:	L M H Evidence:
Notes:			
Scenario 15	L M H Evidence:	L M H Evidence:	L M H Evidence:
Notes:			

Discussion

Ask any teacher who has spent at least 10 years at the same school, "How many administrators have you worked under at this school?" If you come from teaching, or administrative ranks, you won't be terribly surprised if their answer is four or more. Lack of tenure, high accountability, opportunities for advancement, and burnout are only a few of the reasons schools change principals faster than some trees change leaves. Almost a staple of teacher preparation programs is the advice to wait out unpopular administrative policies. Administrators come and go, but faculty and staff are the heart and soul of a school.

Accepting the inevitability of the leadership change, a culture of administrative "musical chairs" can develop. Perhaps it's an attempt to keep supervisory relationships at the professional level so that friendships don't prevent documentation of poor performance. Maybe, the shuffle occurs to prevent stagnation, or to decrease the occurrence of grievances, as the likelihood of the offending administrator being moved to another school is quite possible. Then again, the choice of school administrators to move can be quite voluntary to further a career, or to find a higher degree of security and/or trust with an employer.

Regardless of the cause, the inevitable movement of school leaders leaves schools in a continual state of flux, unless a core of teacher and staff leadership is developed. The greatest legacy leaders can leave behind is that they developed themselves out of their jobs! By creating not just the practice of collaborative leadership, but a true, lasting program of team leadership, the leader has left a durable stamp on the direction of the organization. The impact need not be systematic to make permanent changes on the leadership of the school. One process at a time, such as a collaborative committee for designing an open house, can lead to enduring expectations of staff involvement in decision making that can lead to greater stability.

There has been no major research that indicates that annual replacement of principals improves either student performance or staff morale. Frankly, it's quite easy to intuit that such frequent turnover of leadership can be quite harmful to both. Whether you have been brave enough to newly captain a floundering ship, like the principal in Scenario 14, or you have otherwise found yourself leading a low-performing, low-morale school (or just wish to prevent your school from taking that slide), the decision of which problem to tackle first might not be as difficult as it seems.

If you want to positively impact the performance of the organization, you must first remain in the position long enough to have that impact. All the reforms, all the consultants, all the in-services, and all the mandates in the world will have only a minimal, and fleeting impact (if any) on what actually goes on behind the closed classroom door, *unless* you are able to affect the hearts of those responsible for creating that impact. If you hope to instill a student-centered focus on all aspects of your school, you must begin at the personal level. Develop a genuine relationship with those through whom you get the work done. Show them that you care about them, and only then will you channel the energy necessary to make the desired positive impact on the school. Of course, the measure of your success is up to your personal interpretation of success, but how could anyone think of the principal in the Scenario 14 as anything but a success? She created an enduring structure of teacher-led, renewable energy for improving student achievement.

With all the reports of positive benefits of teacher leadership and empowerment, novice school leaders might be surprised at the all-too-often peer sabotage of teacher leadership efforts (unless, of course, they were subject to such attacks as a teacher-leader, themselves!). Ages of mistrust between teachers and administrators will not be dismissed just because an enlightened administrator decides to appoint a few individuals or committees to the leadership ranks. In fact, the highly structured "hidden" organizational chart seems to strictly enforce the social pecking order. This can easily supersede any imposed professional elevation of rank. You make a good target when standing on a pedestal, and after taking a bull's eye hit, few teachers wish to step up to a leadership role again. The order will be reestablished.

How, then, can you protect your "tall poppies" so their heads are not "cut down to size"? How do you provide a safe learning environment in your classroom, where students are safe to take risks in answering questions, making presentations, and participating in team work? There is a reason why a school leader is called "principal." The principal teacher or "first" teacher has to set the tone for the school, the same way teachers set the tone for the classrooms. When you are in the classroom, you set (preferably, with the students' input) expectations for behavior, teach the desired behaviors, and enforce the expected behaviors (again, preferably with the students' participation).

Why do we expect that running a harmonious school would be any different than running a harmonious classroom? It's not, except that now your students are professional adults. Cultivate and apply the same curiosity and determination you use to develop safe learning environments and student leadership in your classes to your job as principal teacher. Apply the staff's input to your vision of shared leadership. Give them what they want, and then teach them to want more. See that as many people who want leadership training have access to it, especially those who carry any leadership burden. With a deeper understanding of decision making, group facilitation, conflict resolution, legal and ethical issues, not only will the leaders be better equipped for success, potential saboteurs might also cease to undermine.

Self-Assessment

- ◆ Is there a baseline of trust present in your organization?
- ◆ How long is your personal commitment to your current leadership position?
- ◆ Are you more interested in your reputation or your legacy?
- ◆ What do you do to deliberately improve morale on your campus and in your organization?
- ◆ Have you provided leadership skill training to teachers interested in serving as teacher leaders?
- ◆ What have you done to create a positive learning environment in your faculty meetings (and beyond)?

New Agreements

Scenario 16

As you read this passage, focus on the following questions:

- ■ *Is there a point where policies favoring staff have a negative impact on student achievement?*
- ■ *Why can public pressure force opposing groups to renegotiate agreements?*
- ■ *How could training in collaboration help all parties adjust to a flattened hierarchy of decision making?*

Nearly three decades had passed since the high school district had opened a new school, and during that time, it struggled to improve dismal student achievement scores. Both certified and classified associations had gained enviable agreements with administration, yet although it was "a great place to work, it was a bad place to learn." Five years earlier, a dispute between the teachers' association and administration resulted in a "spanking" by the public, demanding an end to the bickering and a commitment to the students. A new school was designed; a school that replaced the two-inch thick agreement with an eight-page compact for collaboration among administration, faculty, and staff. Lines were blurred between ranks, as all employees shared in making decisions for the school. Traditional top-down governance was replaced with an alphabet soup of councils and committees. The chief administration unit, the Educational Action Council, consisted of an elected representative of each association, certified, classified, and administrative. Teachers were not centered on departments. Instead, they were centered on floors, which housed school-within-a-school core curriculum units. Each floor elected a representative to the Professional Unit Committee (PUC), which met regularly to decide issues of school governance. These representatives took issues back to their floors, discussed and debated them, and returned to the PUC meeting to work out consensus on decisions. Frustration ran high at times, as endless meetings cut into work time for all parties, and simple decisions could take months to make.

Scenario 17

As you read this passage, focus on the following questions:

- *Is advice-giving important to the role of a principal's advisory team?*
- *What role does complaining play in teacher empowerment?*
- *When people reject being part of the solution, how can the leader move forward with collaboration?*

It was the first meeting of the Principal's Advisory Team, and the new principal was somewhat confused by the agenda that had been delivered by the chair of the committee. There was no goal, no timeline, and the action items, if you could call them that, appeared to be rambling e-mail messages copied into a single document. The chair called the meeting to order, and the elected members took their seats; the principal mentally rolled up her sleeves to start the work of collaboratively resolving the concerns of the staff. The agenda was read, word for word, one complaint after the other—a virtual laundry list ranging from "I don't like the new science room furniture; I can't control the kids if they sit at the lab tables" to "I don't like the hand dryers in the new bathrooms; we want paper towels!" The principal discussed each issue with the teachers, seeking to remove each obstacle until one item clearly required a collaborative resolution, rather than a maintenance order. "There is inadequate supervision of students in the cafeteria." All of the security personnel, plus all administrators were on duty during lunch, yet the teachers wanted more. "What solutions do you think would solve this problem?," the principal asked the Advisory Team. "Oh, we're not here to solve problems," they said almost in unison, "we're here just to complain." Doing her best to keep her jaw from dropping, the principal couldn't believe that this advisory committee fully rejected the opportunity to be involved in the solution side of school management. Having already used all personnel available to supervise the lunch hour, yet needing to appease the teachers' desire for more, she designed a teacher duty schedule after consulting the union contract.

Scenario 18

As you read this passage, focus on the following questions:

- *Why is it necessary to change the manner of evaluating leaders when they officially share their power?*
- *What is the leader's incentive to respect the group decision-making process when they stand alone at evaluation time?*
- *To what degree should collaborative behavior be part of a new evaluation document under shared-leadership organizations?*

Although the process for running the school had changed from top-down to collaborative decision making, the process for evaluating personnel had not. The principal found himself in constant conflict with the decisions made through staff consensus. Often, he would deliberately alter the implementation of the decision or side step the process, stating it was "easier to ask forgiveness than permission." Justification for his actions was easy, it wasn't the staff, or even the top council that stood accountable for how the school was run. It was him. He stood alone at "judgment" time, being evaluated with the same administrator evaluation instrument used during the good old top-down management days. The principal's evaluation held only the principal accountable for decisions made by the staff and leadership council, even if he disagreed with them. He figured, "when they give up the comfort of 'tenure' and stand fully accountable to the superintendent like I do, then I might consider sharing my power with them."

Figure 3.2. Analysis Table 6

Directions: For each of the preceding scenarios, circle the level of trust between the leader and others with an "L" (low), "M" (medium), or "H" (high) in the appropriate column. If helpful, note any evidence for your rating. Repeat this process to rate the effectiveness of the working environment and the overall outcome of the situation. Finally, make note of any thoughts that you can apply to your own leadership in the Notes column. You should use these later to build your action plan.

	Trust between Leader and Others	Effectiveness of Working Environment	Overall Outcome
Scenario 16	L M H Evidence:	L M H Evidence:	L M H Evidence:
Notes:			
Scenario 17	L M H Evidence:	L M H Evidence:	L M H Evidence:
Notes:			
Scenario 18	L M H Evidence:	L M H Evidence:	L M H Evidence:
Notes:			

Discussion

It is an ugly fact that during annual negotiations (or meet and confer) adults can sometimes become so embroiled in seeking fairness (not to mention advantage) that they forget the primary purpose of their organization is to educate students. When tensions run so high that the students feel the negative atmosphere, or an organized "blue flu" leaves students under the care of substitutes, the concept of staff empowerment has backfired. We must find a way to keep our mission above our decisions.

Just as a police officer is often required to direct traffic through a clogged intersection, an outside authority might be needed to step in and direct staff and administration to "play nice" when competing for limited resources. Ultimately, a school district is directed by vocalization of the board's constituency. Members of that constituency who have children attending school in the district might not have enough voice to force their direction. However, when combined with the mass of nonparent constituents, their voices can be heard, loud and clear. How do these voices unite, and what fuels the mandate to stop squabbling and start educating? The short answer is the media. The media easily shapes public opinion and public sympathies. The media can present teachers as greedy, money-hungry, self-centered fiends, just as quickly as they can paint the same image for school administration. When the media doesn't favor one side over another, public pressure to renegotiate agreements, putting students first, can redefine roles and goals of school leadership.

Imagine that your school district has just received a very clear mandate by voters to put their differences behind them and put students' interests in front of them. All parties agree that prolonged and public power struggles are to no one's favor. Best practices in modern leadership hail collaborative models as exemplary, so it is agreed that collaboration will be mandated for school administration. This is the crossroads of creating either a truly spectacular, student-centered, empowered school *or* descending into disorder and chaos. Which system emerges depends on the crucial element of collaborative leadership. If the collaborative process is to succeed long-term, effective and ongoing training in cooperation, consensus making, and supporting group norms must be in place. The strength of this particular teachers' association proved no match for the power of the media and public opinion; it opened the door to a new leadership model. After moving to the point that the willingness to operate under shared power primes the leadership pump, neglect in teaching these formally oppositional groups to work together would be almost criminal.

Another ugly fact of life is that people like to complain. Even nice people find themselves enjoying a good gripe every now and then. Negativity breeds negativity! Without injection of positive energy, the negative charge flows unhampered. If it is the leader's intention to be a true servant leader, such a climate can spell doom for him or her, unless he or she takes a deep look at what it means to be a servant leader. A servant's efforts enable the master to accomplish greater heights than possible without that assistance; he or she removes drudgery from the way of greatness. It would be a short-employed servant who allowed his or her master to cause harm to him or herself. The same is true for a servant leader. Little, to no positive results occur when input becomes a culture of complaints. A good servant would clean up the master's environment, and that is the task for a good servant leader as well.

To be effective in removing obstacles that put the brakes on student achievement, a servant leader must be savvy to what those obstacles are. Going on one's gut feelings in this matter is not recommended. Ask! Take an active role in a continual collection and analysis of data from every source, particularly your staff and students. If you want to remain a servant leader, rather than a doormat, the key element to such advisories must be that of positive energy flow. Whether suggestions come from an elected counsel of school representatives or the old standby, suggestion box, the tone has to be constructive, not destructive. Insist that every complaint be accompanied with at least one solution. Suggestions need not be brilliant, outstanding, or even usable, but they should indicate an effort to be part of the solution, rather than just being a source of negative energy.

The first lesson we learn when we are taught to "play nice" is what is considered fair. When I was raising my sons, I would have one of them divide a piece of cake (or peanut butter sandwich, candy bar, or so on; you fill in the blank), but the other would get to choose his portion first (they are both great at math to this day!). Why, then, is it not so easy to include fairness into the agreements that guide collaborative leadership? In our enthusiasm to implement shared leadership, we overlook the need to consider how this impacts the formal evaluation of the leader's performance. If leaders truly embrace the collaborative approach voluntarily, it is assumed that they accept the risk of not having complete control over the outcomes. They are willing to be judged alone, based on the results of shared leadership. This reality can deter a full commitment to the shared leadership approach, especially if such an approach has been mandated. When committing to distributing one's authority to run the school, lobby to alter aspects of your professional evaluation process to account for the fact that you administer with shared leadership. It's not a "piece of cake," it's just like getting to slice it.

Self-Assessment

- Do your union and/or association agreements favor staff at the students' expense?
- During negotiations and/or meet-and-confer, do all parties commit to making student-centered agreements?
- Have all school employees received adequate education in using collaboration?
- Do you have a forum for teachers to express their concerns to management?
- If so, is the forum solutions-oriented? Are the faculty and staff both empowered *and* responsible for making positive changes?
- When presented only with problems, do you resort to taking charge and directing solutions?
- Do you find yourself frequently asking forgiveness of the staff, rather than negotiating permission?
- Is collaboration a criteria for which you are professionally evaluated?

Equitable Resources

Scenario 19

As you read this passage, focus on the following questions:

- *How do district politics impact allocating resources?*
- *What should be the primary concern when distributing school resources?*
- *Does developing interpersonal relationships condone or reduce the role of politics in decision making?*

The overhaul of the school complex was almost complete, leaving the old library vacant and available for new uses. For years, the Junior Reserve Officer's Training Corps (JROTC) program on campus had shared target-practice space with the auto shop, leaving both programs in violation of regulations and safety codes. Many groups competed for getting hold of the library space, and several individual meetings were held with the various parties. The principal considered all proposals for the area and made his decision. He proposed to brick off a "slice" of the room for an indoor air rifle range, and divided the remainder into much needed storage, a community volunteer workroom, and a wet lab for the photography class. He did not seek the assistant superintendent's approval for the plan before it was announced. Several teachers who had wanted to move their classes into the oversized room voiced their disapproval of the decision to the assistant superintendent, who promptly reversed the principal's plan and allocated the space to the complaining teachers.

Scenario 20

As you read this passage, focus on the following questions:

- *What is the connection between instructional decision making and fiscal decision making?*
- *Are effective professional working relationships strained when competing for limited resources?*
- *How can an increase in interpersonal trust improve this ongoing dilemma?*

For years, the department chairs of the high school had met with the principal as an "instructional cabinet" to discuss academic issues at the school. The principal had a great deal of respect for these teachers in regard to their instructional leadership among the faculty. Many school-wide instructional initiatives had been collaboratively implemented and successfully maintained over the years, and a forum of academic integrity prevailed among the group. One major source of contention plagued the cabinet, however. Whenever department budgets were distributed by the principal, no discussion of allocation was allowed. Chairs did not understand the criteria for distribution of funds, and many perceived a sense of unfairness year after year. When her new AP questioned the budgeting practice, the principal told him, "If you want to destroy the cooperation among teacher leaders, throw money into the pit. They will fight bitterly over it, and the animosity spills over into everything they do together." The AP hadn't noticed any indicator that this cabinet wouldn't continue its professionalism in regards to the budget and silently wondered if his principal was correct.

Scenario 21

As you read this passage, focus on the following questions:

- *What role does leading by example play in the outcome of this scenario?*
- *How did the superintendent resolve the financial standoff with the faculty?*
- *Was the act of full disclosure of the budget a ploy or an act of honesty?*

"Just what is the most important use of our limited funds?" the teachers thought, staring at the financial priorities survey in front of them. Negotiations with the teachers' association had arrived at a standoff over an increase in teachers' salaries. This was the third year of the budget freeze, and administration was meeting with all the teachers, classified personnel, and interested members of the community. The superintendent had just presented them with the most honest look at the district budget they had ever seen. Each group was presented the amount of money available to the district, along with a breakdown of fixed costs such as salaries and utilities. Two years ago, the superintendent had refused to accept his guaranteed salary increase, and last year, all other administrators in the district followed his example. Now, they turned to the staff and community to prioritize spending, and identify potential cuts. As survey after survey was tallied across each group, a surprising trend emerged. Increases in teacher salary was only critically important to a small percentage of the faculty; the majority of teachers, support staff, and community members placed instructional supplies and field trips as the best use of district funds.

Figure 3.3. Analysis Table 7

Directions: For each of the preceding scenarios, circle the level of trust between the leader and others with an "L" (low), "M" (medium), or "H" (high) in the appropriate column. If helpful, note any evidence for your rating. Repeat this process to rate the effectiveness of the working environment and the overall outcome of the situation. Finally, make note of any thoughts that you can apply to your own leadership in the Notes column. You should use these later to build your action plan.

	Trust between Leader and Others	Effectiveness of Working Environment	Overall Outcome
Scenario 19	L M H Evidence:	L M H Evidence:	L M H Evidence:
Notes:			
Scenario 20	L M H Evidence:	L M H Evidence:	L M H Evidence:
Notes:			
Scenario 21	L M H Evidence:	L M H Evidence:	L M H Evidence:
Notes:			

Discussion

The *American Heritage Dictionary* defines politics, in part, as "The often internally conflicting interrelationships among people in a society." It is important to keep in mind that "often" and "interrelationships" are key words of this definition. First, because "internally conflicting interrelationships" occur often, it is well worth one's time to understand that politics are inescapable events, especially if one wishes to lead. Second, because politics are based on interrelationships, a leader should welcome the opportunity to continually improve said relationships. Consider that politics are the inevitable processes of dealing with people and groups of people, and that is what leaders enjoy doing. It's only when we assume *all* politics are *dirty* politics that you see leaders decide they should ignore or avoid political behaviors. This can be disastrous to careers and to one's school.

Face it, it's harder to say no to someone you like. It's not impossible, just harder. Provided you, as a leader, have an equal opportunity relational outreach attitude, what is dirty about building relationships? You should have the same genuine concern over how your boss's day is going as you do about how the crossing-guard is doing. If you ignore the power of relationships, you can be certain that others will not. They will build webs of relationships all around you, above, below, and beside you, but not including you. You will be the outsider. Your interpretation of the situation at hand will carry less value than that of someone people trust. So, why would any leader want to avoid building people's trust? Politics simply cannot be ignored.

Just as professional politicians develop and publicize their platforms, school leaders must also see that their stakeholders know what they stand for, especially when it comes to resource and fiscal distribution. The students must be at the center of all such decisions. Petty control issues, turf wars, and even genuine need can be managed when there is no mystery surrounding (1) what *is* available, (2) how division decisions were made, and (3) the "big picture" of how students benefit from the decision. Again, where there is interpersonal trust, there is no mystery.

Hopefully, you have never experienced the pain of watching a close-knit family dissolve into a virtual cat fight over the estate of a departed loved one. I would bet, however, that you know someone who has been through such an ordeal. It is truly unfortunate that money can instantly (and negatively) transform the best relationships into bitter combat. With this in mind, one might seriously consider the advice of the principal in Scenario 20, "Don't ruin your instructional leadership team by giving them control over the budget." This doesn't mean that teachers should be excluded from budgetary input and decision making. It only means you need to isolate the process. Actually, because the budget affects everyone, why not involve everyone? By informing all faculty of the bottom line, you can meet with smaller groups (departments, grade levels, houses, etc.) and determine their needs *and* wants. Take the opportunity to build and nurture your relationship with these people and to understand their requests. Then, bring all the groups together, once they have trust that you, their leader, knows what their needs are, and you have trust that they understand the difference between their needs and their wants. Show them how the final allocation of resources maximizes the coverage of needs, and is fair in addressing wants. It's not dissimilar to a fair and legal will and testament; it keeps the family close knit.

Self-Assessment

- ◆ Do you ensure that your resource allocation decisions are based on the collective needs of the students?
- ◆ Are your interpersonal relationships with school and district personnel strong enough to openly discuss fair, student-centered budgeting?
- ◆ When disagreements arise over distribution of resources, do you address the situation square on?
- ◆ If there appears to be no disagreements over resource allocations, do you personally investigate the feelings of all affected parties?
- ◆ Have you informed your staff of your budget? Do they know the requests made by all departments?
- ◆ Are all parties aware of the criteria for making resource distribution decisions?
- ◆ Did they have a voice in creating those criteria?

Shared Accountability

Scenario 22

As you read this passage, focus on the following questions:
- ■ *Does this case demonstrate shared accountability or only shared praise, if results are favorable?*
- ■ *How does a voluntary action become a traditional expectation?*
- ■ *Why did risking loss of control pay off in such extraordinary results?*

Each of the four APs of the high school was responsible for a specific set of duties. Throughout the year, they met weekly with the principal to review progress on these duties and receive various extra assignments. The AP responsible for instruction and assessment was assigned the open house, a function with notoriously poor turnout across the district. Expectation for the event was equally low within the administrative team meeting. Leaving the meeting, the AP decided to use a committee of faculty and staff to organize this year's open house. Invitations were sent to 8 to 10 individuals who met with the AP and listened as she proposed joint ownership of the success for the event. Never having had input or responsibility for the school's open house, the committee seized the opportunity to make it one to remember. They recommended recruiting a few more key members to the committee, so each faction of the event was led by an "expert." The AP served as a facilitator when the committee developed their vision of the big picture, uncovering stumbling blocks to prior open houses never imagined by administration alone. Excitedly reporting back to the administration team, the AP was reminded that, although they can approach their duties anyway they want, they will be the ones taking the fall if the results are poor. Unhampered, the junior administrator continued with the communal organization of the open house. More than 1,000 individuals, plus faculty and staff, attended the event. Both staff and community were thrilled with the evening. In the following years the committee was expected to continue to be involved in planning and implementing the open house. Voluntarily shared responsibility led to a shared accountability for the event.

Scenario 23

As you read this passage, focus on the following questions:

- *Who is ultimately responsible for the outcomes of any school program?*
- *What message is sent to faculty and staff when program directors account to them the results of their programs?*
- *Does a "final say" constitute shared decision making?*

The school's principal picked up the telephone one day early in July. "Hey, Donnie," he said, with the assurance that she would immediately recognize his voice, "I think I found a good candidate for your world history position. Do you want to give her a call and let me know what you think?" He was talking to the counselor he had appointed to head the school's drop-out prevention program. Close to 300 students who would otherwise fall through the cracks and disappear from the school were rescued by that program every year. The principal kept more than 100 teachers, not associated with this school-within-a-school, satisfied with the smaller class sizes and scheduling flexibility afforded to the program by holding the director (and program members) accountable to the faculty as a whole. Each year, the team prepared the annual report to faculty on the success of the drop-out prevention program. The program director stood in front of her peers each year and presented the results of the program, and each year, the faculty voted to continue the special allocations to the department's mission. "With that kind of accountability," the principal thought as he set down the phone, "Donnie deserves to have the final say on anyone hired for the program."

Scenario 24

As you read this passage, focus on the following questions:

- *Are teacher leaders empowered if they have no positional authority?*
- *How would the potential expert authority of the chairs be impacted by their emotional reaction to the principal's directive?*
- *Are the perceived rewards for serving as department chairs equal to or greater than the perceived costs?*

"I don't care how you get it done, just get it done!" With the principal's words still hanging in the air, the team of department chairs sat in silent frustration as the principal exited the room. She had made it perfectly clear that if standardized test scores did not improve across the board, the lowest performing teachers would be dismissed for lack of performance, and their department chairs would be replaced. How could they be accountable for student performance, as the principal insisted, if they had no power? They held no direct supervisory power over teachers in their department. They had no power over their curriculum or even over instructional resources. Most excelled in teaching their own classes but had no idea on how they could impact the way their department taught. "Well," Mr. Jones finally offered, "we might lose all this," gesturing to the stressed expressions and piles of additional paperwork. "But we're tenured, and we know how to teach. Who are they really going to fire if scores don't improve?"

Figure 3.4. Analysis Table 8

Directions: For each of the preceding scenarios, circle the level of trust between the leader and others with an "L" (low), "M" (medium), or "H" (high) in the appropriate column. If helpful, note any evidence for your rating. Repeat this process to rate the effectiveness of the working environment and the overall outcome of the situation. Finally, make note of any thoughts that you can apply to your own leadership in the Notes column. You should use these later to build your action plan.

	Trust between Leader and Others	Effectiveness of Working Environment	Overall Outcome
Scenario 22	L M H Evidence:	L M H Evidence:	L M H Evidence:
Notes:			
Scenario 23	L M H Evidence:	L M H Evidence:	L M H Evidence:
Notes:			
Scenario 24	L M H Evidence:	L M H Evidence:	L M H Evidence:
Notes:			

Discussion

There really is no true leadership without accountability. When you set out to inspire, direct, or guide others, it is really up to you to get them to your destination. If teachers and staff are truly to take leadership roles within the school, what then prevents them from sharing accountability for their outcomes? Praise is a nice thank you for a job well done, but what about the deeper, intrinsic drive to have a meaningful impact on the school's performance? How do you stoke an interest in leadership into a personal passion for group success? Accountability! With personal accountability on the line, the competitive nature of humanity emerges and inspires people to greater and greater heights.

This is the essence of leading from behind: inspiring others and making it possible for them to reach their potential beyond what they would have done without your influence. If you want to reach your expectations, you can hold tight control over school operations, but if you want to far exceed those expectations, tap into to the leadership capacity of all those around you. You might not have the means, or desire, to use the formal evaluation process to hold your staff leaders accountable for their leadership contributions, but this does not mean they can't, or shouldn't, be accountable. Peer-to-peer reporting goes a long way in developing the deep intrinsic sense of meaningful accountability that is necessary to truly empower a staff to make a positive impact on the school. In anticipation of this accountability, leaders hone their efforts, so a culture of peer leadership can thrive.

Until the concept of shared accountability works its way into the principal evaluation process, ultimately the principal is accountable for the school's performance. This makes it incredibly tempting to fall back onto the power of positional authority when stakes are high. Unfortunately, positional authority is not the most inspiring thing to work under. The best employee performance you can expect is what you direct, and you'd be lucky to get that. The referent and expert powers freely given to leaders who qualify evaporate in the vicinity of directive or coercive behaviors. The magic of leadership dies and is replaced, in the best case, with obedience (you really don't want to fully understand the worst case!). Instead, maintain and develop the interpersonal relationships with all your staff, as well as your leaders. Empower your leaders with the tools and resources they need to serve fully in their expert role. Nurture their passion for serving and see that they feel the rewards for their efforts, and you will have a sustainable and renewable source of continual servant leadership throughout your school.

Self-Assessment

- Are you required to share responsibility and accountability with your faculty and staff? Do you do so voluntarily?
- How often do you sacrifice total control over an outcome to tap into the leadership potential of your staff?
- Do you give away all praise for a job well done to those who collaborated with you?
- What degree of final say do you give to your teacher leaders?
- To what degree do you hold teacher-leaders accountable for their leadership?
- Do you provide clear direction for your teacher leaders?
- In what ways have you officially empowered your leaders to successfully accomplish their task?
- What steps do you take to remove obstacles to their success?

Having completed the analysis charts for all topics in this chapter, focus on your Notes column for each. Use your notes to complete this action plan (Figure 3.4) for applying these ideas to your own leadership style.

Figure 3.4. Action Plan 2

Teacher Leadership Needed to Provide Stability

Goal: (Describe the resilient structure of teacher leadership you want your campus to have, long after you're gone.)

_____

_____

_____

Assessment: (How and when will you measure your progress toward your goal?)

_____

_____

_____

Action Steps:

1._____

_____

_____

2. _____

_____

_____

3. _____

_____

_____

_____

New Agreements

Goal: (Describe the new agreements to be drawn to establish and maintain a viable teacher-leadership presence on your campus.)

_____

_____

Assessment: (How and when will you measure your progress toward your goal?)

_____

_____

Action Steps:

1. _____

_____

_____

2. _____

_____

3. _____

_____

_____

Equitable Resources

Goal: (Describe the process and outcomes of the teacher-led, student-centered budget for distributing resources on your campus.)

_____
_____
_____

Assessment: (How and when will you measure your progress toward your goal?)

_____
_____
_____

Action Steps:

1._____
_____
_____

2. _____
_____
_____

3. _____
_____
_____
_____

Shared Accountability

Goal: (Describe the level and method of teacher-leader accountability.)

_____
_____

Assessment: (How and when will you measure your progress toward your goal?)

_____
_____
_____

Action Steps:

1._____

_____

_____

2._____

_____

_____

3._____

_____

_____

_____

4

It's a Team Thing

Now that we've identified our leadership limitations, as well as ways to build strong, trusting relationships, we need to tap into the collective knowledge of our staff. This chapter focuses on creating a network of leaders within the school, capable of successfully addressing key school functions. Professional development, teacher accountability, school safety, and "special" programs are all areas best led through close collaboration among faculty. Let's see what lessons we can take by examining the following stories in each of these areas.

Professional Development

Scenario 25

As you read this passage, focus on the following questions:

- *To what degree was the timing of this staff development meeting considerate of teachers' schedules?*

- *What actual item produced any "development" in anyone?*

- *What conclusions can you draw about the "value" placed on staff development by this administration? This faculty?*

It's five thirty in the morning as the first-year teacher drops off her two children at the daycare center and rushes to her school library for the monthly one-hour staff development meeting scheduled for six. Arriving too close to the starting time to get the good seats in the back of the room, she makes her way to the front row, picking up an agenda along the way. Shortly after, the AP starts the meeting with jokes about the football team's performance, followed by details about an upcoming pep assembly. The counselor follows this with 10 minutes of discussion on an upcoming student survey. Assigned spots for the parking lot are mentioned, followed by 15 minutes of angry sentiments on how parents have interfered with teacher parking by dropping students off in the wrong area. The teacher looks at her watch and worries about getting to her classroom in time to prepare for class; the principal steps up and begins to describe the accreditation process for the year. When the first bell for students interrupts him, the teacher runs to class, only to find her class already waiting impatiently outside the door.

Scenario 26

As you read this passage, focus on the following questions:

- *Is the value of "taking roll" worth the cost of lost in-service time?*
- *In what way does this in-service honor teachers' valuable time? Devalue it?*
- *How can individualization of staff development support a school-wide initiative?*

A long, weary line of teachers file into the staff development room at two twenty-five in the afternoon. The in-service is scheduled to start at two thirty, but the line is moving slowly, as administration "takes roll" by having teachers sign for agendas and materials. The football coach jokes and visits with his peers, but the seriousness in his eyes hints that his thoughts are elsewhere. It's two forty-five by the time the faculty is fully seated, although the "instructional coach" has been presenting background information for more than 10 minutes. This is going to be a "hands-on" workshop, producing a "guided-reading organizer" to use in the classroom. The coach fails in his attempt not to roll his eyes, as he considers how to apply this teaching method to his physical exercise course load. Although many teachers seem genuinely interested in the topic, the coach is not alone with his concerns. A silent defeat hangs over the table where these teachers gathered, grudgingly producing the minimal work necessary on the "worthless" project to be dismissed and return to their "real work."

Scenario 27

As you read this passage, focus on the following questions:

- *How does collaborative, representative work increase the overall applicability of the professional development plan to the staff's needs?*
- *What role do data-based decisions make in creating a professional development plan?*
- *Why would a combination of required and optional in-services be expected to be easily approved by the staff?*

The five members of the "professional development committee" are wrapping up a long, but productive day prior to the beginning of the school year. Three teachers, elected at large by the faculty, the "peer coach", and the assistant principal form the committee responsible for creating the scope and sequence of the professional development plan for the year. Folders of teacher evaluation data, student assessment data, school vision and mission statements, and faculty surveys have been cross-analyzed and boiled down into charts and tables of professional development ideas. The scope includes flexibility of choice for many strands of in-services, as well as some required sessions designed to continue the school-wide initiatives that support the school vision. A professional development catalog has been drafted, including brief descriptions of each session including objectives, content, and methodology of the in-service and dates offered. The committee is confident that the faculty will approve this year's professional development agenda when they return to school next month.

Figure 4.1. Analysis Table 9

Directions: For each of the preceding scenarios, circle the "level of teacher involvement" with an "L" (low), "M" (medium), or "H" (high) in the appropriate column. If helpful, note any "evidence" for your rating. Repeat
this process to rate the level of the leaders' "consideration to teachers"
and the "overall outcome" of the situation. Finally, make note of any
thoughts that you can apply to your own leadership in the "Notes" column. You should use these later to build your action plan.

	Level of Teacher Involvement	Consideration to Teachers	Overall Outcome
Scenario 25	L M H Evidence:	L M H Evidence:	L M H Evidence:
Notes:			
Scenario 26	L M H Evidence:	L M H Evidence:	L M H Evidence:
Notes:			
Scenario 27	L M H Evidence:	L M H Evidence:	L M H Evidence:
Notes:			

Discussion

You've moved out of your classroom and into administration to make a positive difference to your school. Professional development is probably your best opportunity to do so. Take a close look at your year-long professional development plan. You don't have a year-long plan? That could be problem number one. Chances are your school is suffering from last-minute approaches to staff development and lack of adequate budgeting. Respect is soon lost for school leaders who continually disrespect the value of teachers' time by requiring that they sit through staff meetings that could easily be handled with an e-mail or memo. The same is all the more true for an administrator who confuses or ignores the difference between staff meetings and professional development sessions. They must be kept separate. Respect the role of professional development. You are dealing with teachers; they know good teaching when they see it, and you're on stage!

If you do have a plan, ask yourself, "Who developed our year-long professional development plan?" If teacher representation is not evident, this is a red flag demanding attention. If there was teacher participation, but it wasn't truly reflective of the teachers, you have another red flag. Do in-service objectives apply to all teachers or just to some? Building "choice" into your plan allows teachers to select specific workshops to serve their needs. This improves engagement, morale, and school-wide instruction (not all courses *should* be taught the same way!). Look at the scope and sequence of the year-long plan. Can you highlight where teachers' needs are being met? If your answer is "yes," then good for you; if not, it's back to the drawing board. Meeting the *in-class* needs of your teachers is the goal of your professional development plan, so examine the objectives for each planned session. Do they align with data describing those needs, such as teacher evaluations, student assessments, and faculty surveys? If your response is "yes," again, good! If it is not, it's not too late to fix that.

Assuming that your professional development plan has been carefully planned and customized to meet teachers' needs, the final show of respect for its importance is in the logistics. If you truly expect teachers to be able to absorb the information being presented, you must remove as many distracters from their attention as possible. This means you have to avoid scheduling in-services when it is most convenient for administrators, and focus instead on the best time for teachers' learning. In other words, if it is important, you have to make time for it. This doesn't mean squeezing it in before the first-hour bell, or holding it when teams and clubs are scheduled. Creating bottle necks on entering the in-service, by "taking roll" or handing out materials, is just as distracting to teachers as it would be to a classroom of students. Think instead, how can we hold teachers accountable for participating while maximizing the time we have available? Manage the in-service the same way you expect the best classrooms to be managed. Focus on teacher engagement, and then you've capitalized on the respect you can show for professional development.

Self-Assessment

- ◆ "Do you "squeeze" "administrivia" into staff development time?
- ◆ Are you accountable to teachers for the success of staff development?
- ◆ Do you model your own professional development plan (including your progress) for your staff?
- ◆ Are staff development sessions planned in advance for the whole year?
- ◆ How was the budget for your plan decided? Were teacher representatives involved?
- ◆ Have you analyzed the scope and sequence of your plan?
- ◆ Was the plan (and analysis) done in isolation or with a committee?
- ◆ Do you collect feedback from the teachers on each staff development session?
- ◆ How do you respond to that feedback?

Leading with the Teachers

Scenario 28

As you read this passage, focus on the following questions:
- *How do teachers know what is happening in other classrooms?*
- *Is it fair to assume teachers condone poor teaching?*
- *How can you use peer pressure to improve teacher performance?*

A veteran principal, skilled in the "good old network," and a new AP, insecure in his leadership style, are the only faculty "supervisors" available at this small rural school. The AP conducts most of the teacher evaluations and has found the faculty to be conscientious and competent teachers with the exception of Mr. Smith. Despite all his efforts to develop Mr. Smith, the AP sees no improvement and actually sees something quite to the contrary. Recently, while observing another teacher's classroom, Mr. Smith burst into the class, yelling at a student who had looked into the window of his classroom while on a restroom pass. Students frequently complained that Mr. Smith "leered" at them. Furthermore, several parents had complained that they felt their children in his class were not being taught what was necessary to pass the state graduation examination. One afternoon, the top two union representatives came to the AP and requested to talk "off the record" about Mr. Smith. In response to them being told he couldn't discuss a teacher's performance with them, they said, "but we can, and you can listen." Their laundry list of complaints about Smith's performance made the AP wonder how they had such a clear picture of what happens in other teachers' rooms, but he only replied, "If I were to put any teacher on an improvement plan, it requires the principal's approval. I can tell you that I've asked for a few but only get told that the union will fight us on it." The representatives looked him straight in the eye and said, "Us? We only require that a fair process is used, we don't protect bad teaching. Besides, it's your job to do the unpleasantness of removing poor teachers. We don't ask that they be left in the classroom." The conversation was conveyed to the principal, who begrudgingly signed the improvement plan. The teacher, however, refused to sign it, and resigned on the spot.

Scenario 29

As you read this passage, focus on the following questions:
- *How was the first math teacher's performance rewarded and reinforced?*
- *Is administrative directive or viewing another teacher's performance more likely to develop teachers professionally?*
- *What qualities make that a good method for developing teachers?*

The same AP continued to work with this faculty, to develop a continual improvement philosophy regarding instruction. With only five years of teaching under his belt, his confidence in developing teaching skills in others hinged largely on identifying teachers who excelled in specific principles and referring struggling teachers to them for assistance. On a single day's observation, the AP observed a math teacher in an English as a second language (ESL) classroom, teaching required definitions by demonstrating the properties through examples on the board, and having students discuss in pairs what the examples had in common. Each pair shared their ideas, and the teacher compiled their observations into a single definition for the concept. This was followed by a second round of examples to refine the definitions. Finally, the definitions were applied to seatwork by individual students with great success. The next class period sent the AP across the hall to another math teacher's lesson on the same definitions. This teacher stood at the overhead projector and required students to copy down the definitions of the terms as he wrote them out. Students complied and then were assigned to the same set of problems as the previous class. Students struggled or were off-task for the rest of the class. The next period found the AP in a history class, and definitions were being covered in that class, as well. The method used by the second math teacher was used, with similar results. Although the AP had never even thought of giving "definitions" the way the first math teacher had, he knew this was highly effective teaching. In conference with that teacher, he praised the teacher's use of the strategy, and identified the evidence of its effectiveness. He then asked if it would be okay for him to refer other teachers to her classroom to see how she teaches definitions. She agreed, and both the other two teachers were referred to her. At first, the social studies teacher didn't understand what he could learn from a math teacher, but after meeting with her, the social studies teacher enthusiastically embraced the cross-content learning experience.

Scenario 30

As you read this passage, focus on the following questions:

- *What is the best way to spread a positive teaching practice?*
- *How does emphasizing "teaching" over "content" increase the number of teacher leaders on campus?*
- *Can a school afford to rely solely on the teaching innovations introduced by administration?*

"But I teach science; what can I learn from the band teacher?" a teacher complained in response to the AP's suggestion. Reflecting on his observation of the teacher's classroom, unduly heavy in special education students, and overcrowded to boot, the AP thought, "Plenty." The band teacher's fifth-hour class was scheduled by administration as a "holding" spot for many special education and "at-risk" students. The teacher had turned it into a percussion performance ensemble that was good enough to entertain a presidential candidate and influential senator, as well as sell out three nights of performances for its spring recital. How had that teacher capitalized on the best of the students' characteristics, while neutralizing the worst? The AP wasn't sure but knew that attitude had much to do with it, and as such, he sent as many teachers who struggled in that area to visit the band teacher. None reported anything but inspiration from the event.

Figure 4.2. Analysis Table 10

Directions: For each of the preceding scenarios, circle the "level of teacher involvement" with an "L" (low), "M" (medium), or "H" (high) in the appropriate column. If helpful, note any "evidence" for your rating. Repeat this process to rate the level of the leaders' "consideration to teachers" and the "overall outcome" of the situation. Finally, make note of any thoughts that you can apply to your own leadership in the "Notes" column. You should use these later to build your action plan.

	Level of Teacher Involvement	Consideration to Teachers	Overall Outcome
Scenario 28	L M H Evidence:	L M H Evidence:	L M H Evidence:
Notes:			
Scenario 29	L M H Evidence:	L M H Evidence:	L M H Evidence:
Notes:			
Scenario 30	L M H Evidence:	L M H Evidence:	L M H Evidence:
Notes:			

Discussion

Like a music conductor, your job is to coordinate the talent held by your staff and tie it together toward a unified goal: classroom success. To do this, you must know your campus, and be able to "knit" strengths across the curriculum. You simply can't do this by yourself. It will take working with your staff, and a staff doesn't always feel like working together. This is prime leadership territory. Teachers generally work in isolation, but in tapping the skills of your faculty, and building their leadership roles, you step outside of the "good worker" role and into true leadership.

How well do you know your campus? Which teachers excel in classroom management, and who are outstanding in using specific teaching strategies? When you recruit these teachers to be observed by other teachers, you both reinforce their expertise and develop authentic models for struggling teachers. Do you know which teachers seek real-life assessment methods for their objectives? It's their dedication to discover authentic evaluation of their subject area you want to replicate in other teachers. How can you do that? Examine the core attitudes in your expert teachers to determine what makes their actions so wonderful and discuss your findings with them. This allows them to articulate what they are doing with those teachers you refer to them.

Many people might believe Mr. Smith's story to be fabricated, "No teacher's union would behave that way." I assure you it happened just as described! However, you cannot expect all teachers' associations to behave in the same manner; in fact, I've witnessed the exact opposite. Do teachers condone poor teaching, or are they offended by it? This is a question answerable by the culture of the school. Peers relate to peers, and they will be affected by what their peers do and believe long before what administration says impacts them. When the culture focuses on maintaining the illusion of power and control over others, it becomes more likely that teachers will ignore, or even cover up poor teaching. However, where teachers are developed into servant-first leaders, they are committed to removing any obstacles to student success. This is why you must learn to lead with, and through, your staff. You simply cannot impact teachers the way other teachers can, but you can influence teachers to have the right impact!

The power of your position comes through the acceptance of your staff. If you expect to be solely accountable for the behaviors of every one of your teachers, you don't need to work on developing the leadership capacity among your faculty. However, if you want to *succeed* in providing a strong, nurturing educational environment for your school, you have to lean on the self-regulating nature of an empowered staff. When staff is truly empowered, it has little patience for "slackers" in the ranks. They mentor or pressure others into maintaining the performance level valued by *their* organization.

It's through building and empowering a faculty to set and maintain the standards of their profession that you will experience true leadership.

Self-Assessment

- ◆ Do you know the strengths of your staff?
- ◆ Have you built opportunities for staff to share those strengths with others?
- ◆ Do you trust teachers to make professional decisions based on your school vision and mission statements?
- ◆ Are you willing to share accountability for decisions made by your teachers?
- ◆ Have you discussed your concerns regarding shared accountability with your teachers?
- ◆ How many teachers have you inspired to conduct research on campus needs?
- ◆ Are their results used to further school improvement?

School Safety

Scenario 31

As you read this passage, focus on the following questions:

- ■ *What is the key to maintaining peace in this case?*
- ■ *In what ways did administration serve the school community this day?*
- ■ *In what ways was leadership shared with teachers this day?*

Tension on campus was high all day. Gang violence from the neighborhood had exploded the night before, and school administration was working closely with local police in apprehending suspects and preserving order on campus. The principal sent a brief e-mail to several coaches, asking them to make a presence during lunch and after school. It wasn't necessarily the relatively large frame of these teachers that spurred the principal's request. Their relationship with so many of the students in the school commanded deep respect. Throngs of students passed the day without incident, as administration, coaches, and other "motivated" teachers spent any and all free time among the student body.

Scenario 32

As you read this passage, focus on the following questions:

- *What emotion indicates that the dean needed to reach beyond his own abilities to make a positive impact on teachers experiencing discipline problems?*
- *Did the teacher demonstrations address the lesson with sensitivity? With purpose?*
- *Could an administrative directive accomplish the same objectives?*

Frustrated with the amount of discipline referrals hitting his office by a small percent of teachers, the dean of students decided to approach the matter at a staff meeting. Having analyzed the referrals, he asked teachers who excelled in classroom management to perform related scenarios for the staff. The first reenactment addressed the situation as it occurred for the referral. A second rendition handled the situation using the strategies used by these master teachers. Although no names were revealed, it was clear to certain teachers that many other teachers were able to successfully "manage" the behavior of the very same students.

Scenario 33

As you read this passage, focus on the following questions:

- *What initial action allowed administration to prevent this tragedy?*
- *Does administrative response impact how seriously rumors are taken?*
- *Had the reporting teacher not felt her voice was valued, would she be likely to report the rumor?*

"And to think," the principal shared with her AP, "the result of this long, hard day's work by all of us resulted in absolutely nothing." "Yes," agreed the AP, "good job!" Earlier in the day, a teacher had overheard two students discussing a fight at a party the night before, and how the "cousins" of one combatant would make a "road trip" to resolve the issue during the homecoming dance tonight. The rumor was reported to administration, who contacted police for information, and both authorities used their lawful investigation methods to confirm the plan. Working together, the threat was confirmed and diverted through canceling the dance, and securing the game with an increased police presence. Before half-time, those police informed the administrators that the gunfight had been relocated and intercepted.

Figure 4.3. Analysis Table 11

Directions: For each of the preceding scenarios, circle the "level of teacher involvement" with an "L" (low), "M" (medium), or "H" (high) in the appropriate column. If helpful, note any "evidence" for your rating. Repeat this process to rate the level of the leaders' "consideration to teachers" and the "overall outcome" of the situation. Finally, make note of any thoughts that you can apply to your own leadership in the "Notes" column. You should use these later to build your action plan.

	Level of Teacher Involvement	Consideration to Teachers	Overall Outcome
Scenario 31	L M H Evidence:	L M H Evidence:	L M H Evidence:
Notes:			
Scenario 32	L M H Evidence:	L M H Evidence:	L M H Evidence:
Notes:			
Scenario 33	L M H Evidence:	L M H Evidence:	L M H Evidence:
Notes:			

Discussion

Is school safety limited to fights on campus and bomb threats? Certainly not. Safety issues exist throughout the school, which should provide a comfortable learning environment with clean, functional facilities and prevention of open violence on campus. Students are enclosed in classrooms for close to six hours a day. It is no wonder that much of a school's climate is based on what occurs within the classroom. When diversity in learning styles is ignored, or inadequate planning of lessons results in bored or frustrated students, trouble erupts. Students lash out against the teacher, against each other, or against school property. If students suffer from unresolved emotional issues, drug abuse, or other "outside" factors, teachers are stressed from trying to maintain a safe learning environment for the rest of the class.

Regardless of the stimulus, the results of student misbehavior are class disturbances and office referrals. When a teacher's main resolution of class disruptions is sending the student to the office, it doesn't take long until they have stripped themselves of their ability to control the class on their own. Most discipline referrals come from the same few teachers, and unfortunately, that results in a tendency for administration to dismiss behavior problems stemming from those teachers' classes. To support both the teacher, and the students in their class, it is important that teachers accept their need to develop better classroom management, rather than expect "better" students. This is a lesson an administrator cannot teach. This is where leading from behind is critical to the teacher's development. By involving their peers, the struggling teacher begins to understand that other teachers are able to manage classes with the same students. If most discipline referrals are coming from a few teachers, use the other teachers as your primary source of leadership in classroom management!

A common tool to improve student behavior used by all educators is proximity, making a physical presence known to the students who might be deviating from desired behaviors. This practice is just as useful outside of the classroom as it is inside. In our post-Columbine environment, it is more important than ever to maintain peaceful student behavior on campus. Nevertheless, as school populations continue to increase it becomes more difficult to do this. How can we subdue unruly student behavior on campus? Proximity. Proximity to whom? Administrators? Yes, and no. Yes, when students recognize and see alert administrators around campus, their behavior improves. No, when there are too many students and too few administrators to make a strong presence. So, how can we increase the level of proximity? Bring out the coaches who know vast numbers of students through their teams (I won't disagree that the physical size and confidence demonstrated by many coaches aids in the desired impact). Bring out highly involved and respected teachers who know crowds of students through clubs and activities. This involvement by teachers does not release administration and security personnel from making a strong presence on campus, daily. It just adds a secondary, effective layer of protection in keeping students in-line, especially during stressful circumstances.

How sensitive is your school to rumors? Is there an overall sense of shared responsibility for campus safety, or is administration counted on to maintain order? If teachers have never been enlisted to share this load, your school is missing a key component in providing for a safe school. Teachers are on the front line, and develop the closest relationships with students, and are therefore, very likely to overhear (or be taken into confidence) rumors that could lead to danger for students. What relationship would the teachers need to have with administration to promptly pass this information forward to them? When administration presents the appearance of total control and authority, it is quite possible that a teacher believes administrators would already have the information in question. They might also feel that reporting just a rumor, or something they overheard, wastes administrative time. However, when teacher input is highly valued in all areas, it is natural for teachers to pass rumors on to administration. By acting quickly and providing feedback to teachers on the outcome, you are nurturing the spirit of shared accountability for school safety in the staff.

Self-Assessment

◆ Do teachers freely volunteer to make a "presence" on campus during critical times?

◆ Is the school lunch schedule designed to support teaching and learning or to accommodate administrative needs?

◆ Are teachers involved in analyzing discipline referral patterns or developing solutions to those patterns?

◆ Do you have a process for regular input about the campus climate from teachers and staff?

◆ How are teachers and staff responsible for school safety?

◆ Are teachers provided prompt feedback on rumors or safety issues?

◆ When you provide feedback on rumors, do you word it so as to not spread additional fear to staff who might not have heard of the rumor originally?

Special Programs

Scenario 34

As you read this passage, focus on the following questions:

- *What possible reasons might have resulted in these classrooms being out of legal compliance for years?*
- *What action resulted in instant teamwork?*
- *What role did assigning responsibility play in cementing this teamwork?*

New to the district and building, the principal visits a special education department meeting. Familiar with special education law, yet far from expert in the area, she asks the team questions about the physical setup of the community skills classroom. A flood of information ensues. The school, it is charged, has been out of compliance with the law for years. A brief tour supports the claims, although the principal cannot identify the inadequacies. A conversation with the head of maintenance and two phone calls corrects the physical problems. The team was requested to take responsibility for monitoring and reporting all compliance issues for the special education program.

Scenario 35

As you read this passage, focus on the following questions:

- *Why didn't the AP dictate the testing arrangements for these two special programs?*
- *How many layers of teamwork are represented in this case?*
- *Is there a hint to the motivation behind all this teamwork?*

It was time, once again, for mandated standardized assessment of the students, and the AP sat down with the department chairs of the special education and English language learner (ELL) departments. The AP had been trained with the latest testing requirements, and the department chairs held the up-to-the-minute information of the classifications of their respective students. Together, the three arranged testing rosters and locations that met legal requirements, and satisfied the moral duty to provide the best situation for all their students. The team leaders took responsibility to work with team teachers to notify students of the testing details, and the AP arranged to have all special accommodations and modifications satisfied.

Scenario 36

As you read this passage, focus on the following questions:

- *Did this crisis appear to be the spark for teamwork in this school?*
- *How likely is it that the administration would have identified the problem and corresponding solution without direct input from the department chair?*
- *Why did it take a team to do what was right for these students?*

A challenge to the state law regulating the large ELL population of the school was successful in passing into legislation. The grouping and progressive emersion into English-only instruction used successfully by the high school was now illegal. The ELL department chair worked closely with school administration, instructing them on the consequences of the new law, as well as providing clear "loopholes" that could be used to maintain the current successful structure to the program. Parents, mostly monolingual Spanish speakers, would have to come to the school and sign a "waiver" of the law, requesting that their child continue instruction under the current system. Department teachers designed community meetings, culturally appropriate invitations, translation services, and activities, and administration arranged logistics for the series of meetings. As a result, the ELLs continued receiving the instruction and support necessary to stay competitive in content courses, while rapidly learning English.

Figure 4.4. Analysis Table 12

Directions: For each of the preceding scenarios, circle the "level of teacher involvement" with an "L" (low), "M" (medium), or "H" (high) in the appropriate column. If helpful, note any "evidence" for your rating. Repeat this process to rate the level of the leaders' "consideration to teachers" and the "overall outcome" of the situation. Finally, make note of any thoughts that you can apply to your own leadership in the "Notes" column. You should use these later to build your action plan.

	Level of Teacher Involvement	Consideration to Teachers	Overall Outcome
Scenario 34	L M H Evidence:	L M H Evidence:	L M H Evidence:
Notes:			
Scenario 35	L M H Evidence:	L M H Evidence:	L M H Evidence:
Notes:			
Scenario 36	L M H Evidence:	L M H Evidence:	L M H Evidence:
Notes:			

Discussion

Even if you are a former special programs teacher, keeping up with the ever changing laws involved on top of your administrative duties would be taxing. If you don't have such a background, are you doomed to hope and pray that your programs are in compliance with the law? You are if you are too proud to acknowledge that those working "under" you might know more about current law and regulations than you do. However, if you've embraced the humility of leadership, you are free to empower your teachers to have a say in what needs to be done for their program. A wise saying warns us to "trust, but verify." This verification should not break down the trust.

Empowering these special teachers to have a voice in how their programs operate does not remove you from your own special leadership role. Your first obligation is to remove obstacles for the smooth function of the program, and let the teachers make their impact on your students. A second obligation is to support the teachers stepping into their new leadership roles by collaborating with them in the direction of the program. This active participation demonstrates respect for the program and acceptance of the liability that comes with it. Leaders find themselves accountable for the results of other people's efforts. This is not, however, license to "grab back" dominance over the programs. Your ability to "lead from behind" is tested here. Do you pass?

It should be clear through the cases examined that teams consist of leadership at every level. Knowledge is not confined to rank (some would argue it runs from it!), and it takes knowledge from multiple perspectives to overcome the challenges faced in education. We cannot expect teachers and staff to pull together, combining their knowledge and skill to overcome a sudden crisis, if there is no foundation for such teamwork in every day matters. The job of servant leaders is to do what is morally right for their people and their organization. Through their example of sharing information, seeking input, and removing obstacles to success, the servant leader prepares members of the organization to step into shared leadership roles. This enables the organization to identify storms on the horizon and address them head on.

Self-Assessment

- ◆ Have you ever made an appointment with lead teachers in special programs to have them teach you specifics of their program?
- ◆ When you encounter "new" information, such as a change in the law, do you "tell" the teachers about it, or do you converse with them about it?

- Do you have a process for regular communication with special program teachers?
- Are lead teachers involved when you make arrangements for standardized testing?
- When you delegate a decision to leaders of a special program, do you feel they are now liable for the outcome of their decision?
- When observing special classes, such as "community skills" or "medically fragile" for severely handicapped students, how do you know what to look for and/or how to advise the teacher?
- Have you ever asked a special needs teacher to give you a related topic to research to better serve their program?

Having completed the analysis charts for all the topics in this chapter, focus on your "Notes" column for each. Use your notes to complete this action plan (Figure 4.5) for applying these ideas to your own leadership style.

Figure 4.5. Action Plan 3

Professional Development

Goal: (What do you want your faculty to say about the professional development on your campus?)

_____

_____

_____

Assessment: (How and when will you measure your progress toward your goal?)

_____

_____

_____

Action Steps:

1. _____

_____

_____

2. _____

_____

_____

3. _____

_____

_____

Leading with Teachers

Goal: (Describe your vision for the role of teachers in developing, nurturing, and monitoring each other.)

_____

_____

_____

Assessment: (How and when will you measure your progress toward your goal?)

_____

_____

_____

Action Steps:

1. _____

_____

_____

2. _____

_____

_____

3. _____

_____

_____

School Safety

Goal: (Describe the roles teachers play in maintaining a safe environment on campus.)

_____

_____

_____

Assessment: (How and when will you measure your progress toward your goal?)

_____

_____

_____

Action Steps:

1. _____

2. _____

3. _____

Special Needs Areas

Goal: (Describe the leadership roles your special needs program teachers will play.)

_____

Assessment: (How and when will you measure your progress toward your goal?)

_____

Action Steps:

1. _____

2. _____

3. _____

The Whole
Kit and Caboodle

The final realm of exerting our influence is interorganizational relation-ships. We have mastered our own limitations, learned to lead through others, and networked our organization to work through collaboration among teams. Now, the organization is ready to function within the greater commu-nity. In this chapter, we will look outside our organizational boundaries and work to reach out to our school community. Your school will have the greatest success building bridges to colleges, employment, and families when it functions as a whole entity.

Addressing Cultural Awareness

Scenario 37

As you read this passage, focus on the following questions:

- *How did in-servicing teachers improve cross-cultural interaction?*
- *Would teachers be likely to make home visits without administrative encourage-ment and training?*
- *In what way was the reputation of the school both the cause and the effect of im-proved cultural relations in this community?*

She definitely drew attention from neighbors as she walked through the gate of the modest home of her student. Dressed profes-sionally, down to the heels and hose, this young white female looked out of place in this inner-city, mostly migrant neighborhood, or barrio, as her students referred to it. She rang the bell, hoping to herself that the Survival Spanish in-service she had participated in at the school would be enough to make her purpose known. The door opened and a middle-aged woman peered suspiciously at the stranger. "Hola, me llamo," the teacher began her rehearsed lines, while wondering how she would be able to understand any response. "Oh!" the woman exclaimed, followed by a string of Spanish the teacher could not follow. "...escuela." Ah, I know that word, school, she thought to herself. "Si. Escuela." she replied, smiling in response to the suddenly warm welcome. The reputation of the local school as a student-centered organization preceded this teacher's home visit, and her attempts to speak in the family's native language was appreciated, if not fully understood. "Angelina, la professora está aquí," the woman called to her daughter while seating the teacher and offering her a glass of fresh lemonade.

Scenario 38

As you read this passage, focus on the following questions:

- *In what way does vocabulary and Freudian slips reveal cultural bias?*
- *Is charm a suitable substitute for corrective action?*
- *Will directives alone be enough to change cultural bigotry?*

The principal shook his head in disbelief. For the second time in less than a year, his assistant principal (AP) was in trouble with the tribal leaders from the large Native American reservation just north of the school. The first time, parents and tribal leaders had made an appointment to tell him about their perceived bias on the part of the AP. They complained that he consistently referred to their children as "those Indians" and had stated in two separate discipline hearings to parents of Native American students that their child's behavior was "completely off the reservation." The principal had smoothed over their concerns with his charm and assurances that he would deal with the assistant so that it would never happen again. True to his word, he talked to the AP. "Jon, you can't be so insensitive. Lose the 'holding down the fort' attitude and treat these kids like you would any others." Confident that his talk had reformed his AP, the principal was shocked at the confession he was listening to now. "You told the president's son that he was a waste of classroom space and didn't belong in school?!" Just then the secretary buzzed in. "The tribal president is on line one for you."

Scenario 39

As you read this passage, focus on the following questions:

- *When deeply embedded attitudes predate an administrator, will enforcing policy be enough to change attitudes and behavior?*
- *Is the AP's anger at administrative changes manifesting in the treatment of students?*

- *What role does mutual frustration of culture classes on the parts of the teacher, students, and administrator feed this problem?*

Her hands trembled with contained rage after her meeting with the principal. Ever since the group of church members who had been home schooling their children turned to this charter organization to help them school the older students, it had been a fight with the administration. No, you can't teach religion. No, take the Jesus picture down. No, put the Bibles away. Then the worst violation of their little school—she was letting any student into the school. Try as she might, she couldn't get this principal to see that these little hoodlums were ruining the school. The paper clutched in her hand should have proved to any sane person that those kids were just not cut out for school. She had carefully marked her seating chart with every off-task moment, every off comment, and every rolled eye from those kids for an entire day. How could that administrator be so obtuse as to imply that she was negatively targeting those students and neglecting her duty to motivate and instruct instead of collecting her data all day! The fault belonged to the students with poor attitudes. She had done nothing wrong by tallying all the tiny misbehaviors today!

Figure 5.1. Analysis Table 13

Directions: For each of the preceding scenarios, circle the level of trust between school and community with an "L" (low), "M" (medium), or "H" (high) in the appropriate column. If helpful, note any evidence for your rating. Repeat this process to rate the level of preparation of the staff to interact with the community and the overall outcome of the situation. Finally, make note of any thoughts that you can apply to your own leadership in the Notes column. You should use these later to build your action plan.

	Trust between School and Community	Preparation of Staff to Interact with Community	Overall Outcome
Scenario 37	L M H Evidence:	L M H Evidence:	L M H Evidence:
Notes:			
Scenario 38	L M H Evidence:	L M H Evidence:	L M H Evidence:
Notes:			
Scenario 39	L M H Evidence:	L M H Evidence:	L M H Evidence:
Notes:			

Discussion

Throughout life's journey, we find moving into unknown territory intimidating to some degree. For some adventuresome types, stepping into the unknown is a challenge to be mastered, a source of great excitement. To the vast majority of folks, however, the thought of being alone in an unfamiliar setting produces various shades of butterflies in the stomach. With the necessity of community involvement at the heart of student success, it is natural for administrators to want teachers to serve as ambassadors to the community. What is unnatural for them, however, is to step into the teachers' role and feel the uncertainty of reaching out to a community which they do not fully understand.

Just as brave adventurers seek the summit of Mount Everest with the help of the Sherpa, moving into any unknown area is instinctively easier with a guide who is familiar with the terrain. Servant leaders wanting their staff to intermingle within the school community and engage with parents would first want to remove obstacles preventing the staff from being successful. When a language barrier exists, this is even more important. It isn't as easy as just encouraging teachers to conduct home visits or call parents frequently. These are relatively simple skills, until a cultural barrier must be crossed. Through language courses, "survival" communication courses, and positive exposure to the community culture, teachers find their Sherpa. Providing teachers the skills and knowledge necessary to appreciate and negotiate a different culture is the servant aspect of leading school–community interaction.

Not so long ago, few people ever imagined climbing the summit of Mount Everest. Today, it is a seasonal industry. Where one person has gone, others will follow. This is the key to moving the school into its community. Allow the adventuresome to pioneer the way, provide the resources necessary for their success. They, in turn, return to serve others as guides into the unknown. Soon, there is no unknown. The community is familiar with the school, and the school is familiar with the community. Like a drop of water in a pond, the impact of just one person can spread wide distances. In terms of building mutual respect among school and community, this is even more apparent. As more teachers reach across the boundaries of the school and interact with the community, the community builds respect for that effort. This opens the door even more and welcomes further interaction.

The elephant in the room, when it comes to talking about cultural awareness, is the fact that some people are bigoted. This bigotry might not always be apparent; it might present itself subtly. In this age of political correctness, cultural differences are openly celebrated, but what happens when we encounter those holding deep resentment or mistrust of other cultures? That topic in itself is another complete book, but for this discussion, we will limit this to how a servant leader would address this hot button.

From the start, I want to make clear that bigotry is not exclusive to any one race or culture. It is an equal opportunity disease of the heart and mind. Furthermore, those who suffer from it are not always aware they have the disease. Their symptoms can be masked to themselves, but evident to others, especially those on the receiving end of the situation. The evidence presents itself through biased language, Freudian slips, altered expectations, and outright rejection of a group based on race or culture. These symptoms are expressed as part of the disease of the mind. A servant leader can counsel those expressing these symptoms, help them develop an improvement plan for their behavior, and monitor the progress made. However, the disease extends to the heart, and it is impossible to truly know the heart of another. For this reason, when cultural bias is discovered, all efforts must be made to eradicate not only the symptoms, but the cause.

As leaders, we take responsibility for the behaviors of others. We cannot afford to ignore the cancer of bigotry in our own organizations. Charm can smooth over one overt occurrence among the ranks, but that should not stand alone. It is futile to command someone to have a change of heart after a life-time of developing personal beliefs. Sometimes, tough love is the best way to serve the needs of those struggling against their own demons. If it is possible, support the professional development plan of an individual suffering from cultural bias with counseling, cultural enrichment, and sensitivity training. These provide treatment to the heart as well as the mind. The alternative is not as sensitive to the employee, as there is no place for bigotry in a safe learning environment.

It is not unusual for a leader to move into an organization with a long-standing culture that has a negative impact on students and the community. Symptoms of such a dysfunctional school environment are more readily observable to an outsider than to those embedded within the culture. So, how can a virtual stranger come into such a system and positively change it? A top-down leader would impose directives to uphold policies and laws, using disciplinary action as the stick to enforce it. Would this be effective? That depends on the level of support the new leader has, but here's the heads up on that: If the dysfunction predates the new leader, it probably has more support than the newcomer has!

This kind of action, however, is not the servant leader way of turning around such a situation. Tension and frustration between administration and staff would simmer under the cover of enforcement, until boiling over when the cover is lifted. When the classroom door is closed, the long arm of the law is temporarily lifted, which leaves students to the whim of what could now be a very angry person. No, confronting an irrational belief system, especially one deeply rooted in an organization, with heavy-handed directives will not produce the most desirable results.

We must work to remove the obstacles separating the existing belief system from the harmonious, child-centered organization we desire. The first step in that direction is to understand the existing belief system. People, and organizations, place an acceptance weight on their beliefs, and the heavier that weight, the more they will struggle to maintain it. When you challenge that belief, you threaten the security of the system; it will fight back. Rather, you need to understand the components of the belief so you can develop a plan to dig the support right out from under it. Attack it one tier at a time with lots (and lots!) of carefully presented counter information. Expect the counter information to be rejected, because it usually will be, because it threatens the belief. Persist in working with large and small groups, as well as at the individual level, to continually re-administer the counter information in novel ways. Over time, the old belief system will bend and eventually break. There is no way of knowing precisely how long the process will take, because of the strength of the belief within individuals as well as the group-think belief. What we do know is that this is the only way to change beliefs at the heart level—the enduring change level. This is the service a true leader can provide to a struggling organization.

Self-Assessment

- ◆ How does your community *feel* about your school?
- ◆ Have you systematically measured your staff's aptitude for interacting with your community?
- ◆ What is your strategy to meet the needs of your staff to empower them in connecting with the community?
- ◆ What is the belief system of your school?
- ◆ Do you have the courage to correct hidden or overt bigotry?
- ◆ Do you have programs in place to educate staff on cultural acceptance?
- ◆ What do you do with individuals who hold strong beliefs that are detrimental to students?
- ◆ Have you used your position to dictate change in the attitude of your staff?

Promoting Parent Involvement

Scenario 40

As you read this passage, focus on the following questions:

- *What role did the grassroots nature of this program development play in its success?*
- *To what degree do communication barriers build negative images toward outsiders?*
- *Why would increased positive contact motivate people to improve their understanding of other cultures?*

Out of the 2,300 students in the school, more than 400 were active in the English language learner (ELL) program. Many others had been exited from the program when their English became proficient. The parents of these students, and others whose children were never in the ELL program, had not developed their English capacity alongside their children. This resulted in communication problems between the school and thousands of parents and guardians. The principal noted that many teachers used the excuse that they couldn't communicate with anyone at many of these homes for not calling when students were struggling in class. She further noted that it was generally assumed that parents of "those" students were not interested in being involved with the school. When the ELL department chair and two other teachers came into the principal's office with an excited glow, she put aside what she was working on to devote full attention to their proposal. "We have a grant opportunity," they began, "that would allow us to fund at least two-year's worth of adult English as a second language courses on campus." Her attention perked, and soon full approval of the class was in place. Over the months since it began, the school noticed the size of the classes increasing. Unexpectedly, the number of parents attending open house, literacy nights, and volunteering on campus also increased. Many teachers noticed that these were the very parents thought not to be interested in being involved with the school, and surprisingly, they requested a course be set up for them—to learn Spanish!

Scenario 41

As you read this passage, focus on the following questions:

- *What role does a shared vision play in developing a plan for any program?*
- *How has the lack of a plan for this program impacted its results?*

- *Why did the grassroots nature of this program development not produce successful results?*

"Sarah, come in here a minute; I want you to meet your new parent volunteer coordinator," the principal said to his AP in charge of Title I funds. Sarah managed to swallow her surprise at this announcement. She hadn't even been told that they were looking for a parent volunteer coordinator. "Bonnie will develop a parent volunteer program. She's funded out of Title I, so you'll be her supervisor, but basically, it's Deb's program." Deb, the instructional coach, had pushed for the position, going over the AP's head to the principal. He decided to avoid any conflict by not mentioning it to the AP until it was a done deal. The following months saw thousands of dollars siphoned from Title I funds to provide an endless list of supplies for the parent volunteer center. Desks, bookshelves, file cabinets, televisions ("to entertain the children while their parents are volunteering!"), Internet-connected computers for parents to hone technology skills and seek jobs ("What?!") were among the bottomless pit of items demanded for the program. The principal took over supervision of the program, and Title I, when the AP questioned these expenditures. Months turned into years, and still no plan emerged for recruiting, training, and using parent volunteers. Perhaps it was a good thing that no parent was ever seen in the parent volunteer center.

Scenario 42

As you read this passage, focus on the following questions:
- *What critical resource did the principal supply to this program that allowed teachers to do the impossible?*
- *Were the parents of these at-risk students truly uninvolved?*
- *Would school or parent consequences, alone, be enough to successfully motivate these students?*

The principal funneled funds from his Title I budget and the dropout prevention fund to pay the salary of a single classified employee. This employee would be housed in the Dropout Prevention office and would monitor hourly attendance of the more than 500 students enrolled in that program. Using student aids to collect attendance sheets from every teacher, every period, the employee tallied each tardy and each absence throughout the day. Calls were placed to the parents of any student missing any class during the day, directly to the parents' work, home, or cell number. Each call was logged, so that teachers from the program could assist during their prep periods and/or after school, until every parent had been notified that the child had ditched a class. This seemingly impossible task became quite possible, as parents (combined with lunch detentions) kept pressure on their at-risk children to attend each class, every day. These same parents had been labeled as uninvolved prior to the constant, personal phone contacts. It was no big surprise to the principal that this program recaptured and graduated more than 90 percent of his dropout students.

Figure 5.2. Analysis Table 14

Directions: For each of the preceding scenarios, circle the level of trust between the school and the community with an "L" (low), "M" (medium), or "H" (high) in the appropriate column. If helpful, note any evidence for your rating. Repeat this process to rate the level of preparation of the staff to interact with the community and the overall outcome of the situation. Finally, make note of any thoughts that you can apply to your own leadership in the Notes column. You should use these later to build your action plan.

	Trust between School and Community	Preparation of Staff to Interact with Community	Overall Outcome
Scenario 40	L M H Evidence:	L M H Evidence:	L M H Evidence:
Notes:			
Scenario 41	L M H Evidence:	L M H Evidence:	L M H Evidence:
Notes:			
Scenario 42	L M H Evidence:	L M H Evidence:	L M H Evidence:
Notes:			

Discussion

One of the defining qualities of servant leaders is their ability to listen. They make no assumptions of how things are; they continually seek information from others to see how things are perceived. Problems of which we might not have been aware often are revealed if we just listen to what is on others' minds. More importantly, solutions we might not have considered are also encountered when listening. Our role as servant leaders is not to sway like grass in the wind to every idea. Rather, it is to deeply listen to the ideas and help bring them to light through further dialog. The difference between a successful grassroots effort and one run amuck is the quality and quantity of involvement. When we share the idea with others it, becomes refined through layers of inspection, reflection, and perfection. In other words, the idea gets better. We develop wide support for the idea and we develop a plan for it together. As servants to the organization, we assist the group to uncover a plan for implementing good ideas. If we gloss over that step and bow to private agendas, what part of "leading" have we done?

Another aspect of being a servant leader is being able to build a sense of community. A community relies on communication to tie it together. When there are barriers to communication, because of language, intent, or method, the community is weakened. If we can't understand each other, we tend to think in terms of "us" versus "them." Those we don't understand become the outsiders and can easily be dehumanized as a group known as "them," "they," and "those" people. This poisonous group think undermines any effort to build a true community. We need to remove this obstacle, but how?

Prior to the Internet Age, we would say we can't know someone if we haven't met them. The easy solution is to bring people together, have them share common experiences, learn to communicate, learn to accept and perhaps value each other's cultures. The first two are quite simple to plan for a school. Hold an open house, academic event, or community celebration. However, if a community doesn't exist previous to these events, it is unlikely that the outsiders will attend. The community remains divided. Why? Lack of communication and appreciation creates disharmony in an organization, so who would voluntarily expose themselves to more of that? Before community can be developed, we have to reach out to understand each other. This requires a combination of exposure to the unknown culture, and supportive education regarding that culture. We need to identify what we observe and understand the reason behind it. As servants to the community, we need to explore how to provide the necessary exposure and education to all sections of the community.

Through our commitment to the personal growth of all those in our school community, we draw that community closer together through mutual understanding. We increase trust among its members. The door is opened to a shared direction for the relationship. In developing a common vision for the school-community interaction, both sides of the relationship support each other. Both sides have their needs satisfied. To do this, both sides need to have a voice in planning where the relationship is going. As leaders, we need to establish regular forums for members of the school community to interact, develop a common vision, and plan for meeting their joint needs.

Providing these forums is just the beginning of the stewardship necessary to meaningfully connect the school with the community. We have to support both sides in reaching out to each other for the benefit of children. If teachers and parents struggle with language barriers, we must remove that obstacle through language classes, translators, or both. We must remain empathetic with both parties and work with each to understand the other. Teachers don't go into education because they hate students, nor do parents have no interest in their children's future. Sometimes, finding a way to communicate together is just the straw that breaks the camel's back for these two groups. A wise servant simply removes that straw, rather than beat the camel. When the obstacles of parent–teacher interaction are removed, the natural desire to help kids succeed can be fully activated at home and at school. It takes both, working together, to support a child through today's world. Our role is to do what ever it takes to allow both groups to work together toward this end.

Self-Assessment

- What obstacles does your staff face when interacting with parents?
- What obstacles do your parents face when interacting with your school?
- Do you have an "open door" policy to entertain new ideas?
- How do you encourage your staff to seek solutions to community issues?
- What does your school do to involve parents with the school?
- What do you do to see that your school's efforts are effectively implemented?
- Do you and your staff have the same vision and goals for parental involvement?
- What have you done to develop that vision?
- How are your funds used to involve parents?

Promoting Community Participation

Scenario 43

As you read this passage, focus on the following questions:

- *Why is it important to consider students and alumni as a critical part of a school's community?*
- *Besides money, what valuable assets can business partners offer a school?*
- *How does this school–business partnership directly benefit students?*

Sitting on the panel in front of her former high school's principal, selected teachers, and business professionals, the 21-year-old education major couldn't believe she would be returning for good in just over a year. The principal had encouraged her to join the Future Teachers club in her sophomore year in high school, and from there, her club sponsor had counseled her through the daunting community college to university transfer process. No one in her family had ever gone to college, which had been the norm for her neighborhood. Now her old principal was determined to hire her as a teacher at her old school. She wasn't alone; other alumni were also planning to return to their old community to teach the next generation. They'd been asked to describe their experiences to the Partners as Teachers organization. The school principal had recruited active business partners for the school. They met monthly for luncheons (sponsored by volunteer partners) at the school to interact with administration, program directors, teachers, and students. The school took their employment needs seriously and worked cooperatively to fill those needs with qualified students. The partners provided financial support and served as an advisory to the school, but now they were prepared to donate even more—their time. A program to train the partners as substitute teachers and secure appropriate state credentials for each had been in place for some time. This meeting was the kickoff of the program, as those certified partners would begin donating their time as substitutes while classroom teachers participated in special staff development opportunities. Students would benefit by having their regular teachers gain extra training and by direct contact with "real life" business professionals from their community.

Scenario 44

As you read this passage, focus on the following questions:

- *In what ways do "just plain fun" activities build a school community?*

- *In what ways do "just plain fun" activities fail to benefit a school community?*
- *What could be added to this event to make it more meaningful in building school community?*

"Was that a positive or a negative experience?" the principal of the small K-12 school asked himself on Saturday morning. In an effort to engage more of the community with the school, a survey had been sent to all addresses in the ward, including businesses and homes asking "What kind of activities would you participate in on school grounds?" Honoring the community's input, the principal arranged a Chicken Scratch dance, after researching the exact expectations for such a social event. The turnout was successful; hundreds of people attended the potluck and dance, which lasted well past midnight. The cost was minimal because partygoers brought all the food and beverages and a local DJ volunteered his time. Faculty and staff brought their families and participated in the fun, although technically, the security guard was on duty. Although fun had been had, on school grounds nonetheless, the principal wondered if it would have any lasting impact on the school.

Scenario 45

As you read this passage, focus on the following questions:
- *Why is it important to the school community for teachers to be directly involved with local businesses?*
- *What is the importance of having several school programs to interact with the community?*
- *How can administration support school-business cooperation?*

It was test day for the state's mandatory standardized test, but the coordinator for the school's School-to-Work program was blessed, not having drawn one of the proctor roles. He spent the morning catching up on the volume of paperwork his position required. Already having spoken to several local industries to set up appointments to discuss partnering with the school, and in particular, his program, the teacher was on the phone with a graduate of the program. Part of his monthly duties included tracking graduates' progress in the post-secondary "real world." Just as he hung up on his former student, smiling at another success story, he heard the familiar click of the principal's shoes ringing through the silent hallways. She stepped into his office with an armful of help-wanted flyers. "Bob, this company just dropped these off at the office," she explained. "They need to fill several vacancies, quick, and I thought you might be able to help them out with some of your students." Bob was flattered, because there were several cooperative learning programs on campus that would just as easily fill the employment needs of the community. "Thanks, Sheila. I'll contact the company and send them several candidates. I'm not familiar with this one." "Yes, it was a new one to me, too," the principal replied. "They're new to the community, and when they joined the Chamber of Commerce, they were told about our school and encouraged to contact us for potential employees." The teacher smiled, appreciating the excellent ground work his principal had done to connect this community to the school.

Figure 5.3. Analysis Table 15

Directions: For each of the preceding scenarios, circle the level of trust between the school and the community with an "L" (low), "M" (medium), or "H" (high) in the appropriate column. If helpful, note any evidence for your rating. Repeat this process to rate the level of preparation of the staff to interact with the community and the overall outcome of the situation. Finally, make note of any thoughts that you can apply to your own leadership in the Notes column. You should use these later to build your action plan.

	Trust between School and Community	Preparation of Staff to Interact with Community	Overall Outcome
Scenario 43	L M H Evidence:	L M H Evidence:	L M H Evidence:
Notes:			
Scenario 44	L M H Evidence:	L M H Evidence:	L M H Evidence:
Notes:			
Scenario 45	L M H Evidence:	L M H Evidence:	L M H Evidence:
Notes:			

Discussion

Looking at a school community, it is easy to identity its members: faculty, staff, parents, and administration. In the business of running a school, it can be easy to overlook the group for whom the whole organization exists, the students. Our students, current and alumni, know the school with an intimacy any other group could not imagine. It's not unusual for the students to have a longer tenure at the school than most of the administration! They tend to have an insight into the behind-the-scenes politics and scandal that is uncanny. If the students are saying it, it's often true.

How then, do we so easily overlook them when it comes to building the connections between the school and its community? The children are the purpose we are in business. They are the reason the community wants (and needs) to get involved with our organization in the first place. We need to tap into the student body with the same interest we use when building partnerships with local businesses and parent organizations. Building the leadership capacity within the children is every bit as important as building that capacity throughout faculty, staff, parents, and business. Furthermore, there is a renewable source of concerned community beating in the chest of our alumni. Who better to recruit for teachers and support staff than those who have experienced the school first hand? Whether current or former students, we can't ignore the valuable contribution of the students to the school community.

Our students are the reason we have a school community in the first place. They are the source of future employees to the businesses within the community, and as such, the businesses are stakeholders in school affairs. Of course they have their businesses to run, and they expect the school to develop the students into appropriate workers. What more could be asked of business than to consume the products produced by the local school? How about money? Organizing a partnership of businesses to support their local schools is often centered on financial donations. It's easy for both parties, and makes the business feel they are giving back to the community. Certainly, extra funds are nice, but are they enough?

If many of our students will be working within our community, do we not need to understand what that community needs? We can develop a forum for our business partners to help build the curriculum and programs that will shape the future of the community. By giving this valuable resource a voice, the commitment to the school grows deeper than just their pockets. When we bring the business community into the school, connecting them directly and meaningfully with teachers and students, the true power of partnership can emerge. Whatever the forum, luncheons, coffee klatches, or evening productions, it is important to allow for input by stakeholders and provide an outlet for involvement. Students have a high level of concern about their future—meeting potential employers is highly valuable to them. Therefore, contact between the two groups is a priority, be it on campus or in the work world. The more direct involvement between business and students you can develop, the better off both groups are. There is no blueprint to copy in pulling this off, only the creativity contained within you, your staff, and your community. Learn together, and don't give up!

As a leader in your school community, you have the ability to inspire other members. You bring people and organizations together and empower them to do what's good for students and the community. You open the doors, and you remove obstacles to this relationship. Your teachers are the real power in the relationship, however. By building their leadership potential, you create a mass of ambassadors for the school. Provide them access to the community relationship and let them forge the bonds that tie the community together. They know their students. Help them to know how those students can benefit the community. The programs you have on campus should be designed to help students be successful in the real world. When the teachers leading those programs have a close interaction with that world, the students will benefit.

However, there is more to building a school community than attending to "just business." How do we connect the greater whole of the community? Current and former students and their parents have certain ties to the school, but what of those community members never connected to the school through children? They pay the taxes that support the school, but they have more to offer than just financial resources. Their attitudes toward the school have direct impact on the quality of the school environment. It makes the difference between enthusiastically packed houses at school sporting events and hundreds of fans cleverly disguised as empty seats. It's the difference between sending a marching band to the Macy's Parade and having it sit at home. The part of your community without direct ties to the school has a huge footprint on the success of your school. How do you involve them?

When the community is invited to the school campus, there are two outcomes if they attend. They enjoy it, or they don't. If they don't enjoy it, they might never be back. If they enjoy the visit, there are two outcomes. They might become more involved with the school in meaningful ways, or they might go home and stay there until the next time they are invited to campus. Your task, as the servant leader, is to inspire them to get involved in the school. When you've shown your guests a good time, they like to reciprocate; to take advantage of this, you need to know what it is you want them to do. If you are a genius, you might have dozens of highly useful ideas that meet both the needs of your school and the community. If you are among the ranks of the rest of us, you might want to ask both parties what they might want. Regardless of the source of your ideas, the important thing is that you provide the opportunities to allow people to express their interests and talents in a way that benefits your community.

Self-Assessment

- ♦ What platforms do your students have in your school community?
- ♦ How many alumni are active within your school?
- ♦ How many businesses do you have a partnership with?
- ♦ Do you know the names of individuals within those businesses?
- ♦ What student-centered projects do you have in place with your partners?
- ♦ How do you get your community active on your campus?
- ♦ How to your community events benefit student achievement?
- ♦ How many teachers serve as ambassadors to your community?
- ♦ What role do you play in connecting community with your school programs?

Working with the Central Office

Scenario 46

As you read this passage, focus on the following questions:

- *Do you imagine this method of acquisition is a new occurrence or a long-running symptom of a dysfunctional system?*
- *How does this lack of shared vision harm students?*
- *Rather than sinking to the level of the "end-rounders," how can the principal negotiate a commitment to enforcing policy?*

"You have got to be kidding me!" the principal thought as she read the assistant superintendent's e-mail. No less than three separate teachers had "end-rounded" the chain of command this week. She was so frustrated that her boss continually allowed, almost encouraged, teachers to bring their budget requests directly to him. This left the principal, and those teachers following the correct acquisition process, holding an empty bag when it came to funding their requests. No matter how many times the two discussed the process, it just felt like the assistant superintendent hadn't had enough of making the type of decisions a principal is responsible for before moving up the hierarchy. "Perhaps," pondered the principal, "it's time for me to go over his head and take this complaint directly to the superintendent."

Scenario 47

As you read this passage, focus on the following questions:

- *How does close communication with the district office mitigate the principal's liability in this situation?*
- *Had there been no legal agreement between the district and the city, how might this scenario be different?*
- *What district resource helps the school's image?*

Although the situation was under control, the principal placed a quick call to the assistant superintendent to let him know about the brief student walkout at lunch. Students were voicing their opinions on immigration issues occurring in the state. The student council had organized a walkout in protest of recent legislation impacting many members of their community. Out of respect, the student body president notified the principal of the school immediately prior to the mass exodus of campus. "They're just heading to the park?," the assistant superintendent asked. "Yes. According to our intergovernmental agreement, during school hours it is under our supervision anyway, so technically they aren't leaving school grounds," the principal replied. "Send as many of your people as possible to provide supervision and security, and I'll get Jim out to you—just in case." Hanging up, the principal contacted the administration team and security by radio, sending them to the park. He was particularly glad that his boss was sending the district's public relations specialist to the campus as he spotted the television helicopter hovering over the park. "Jeanine," he said into the radio, "get the conference room ready for the press. Make them comfortable and let them know our spokesperson will be with them shortly."

Scenario 48

As you read this passage, focus on the following questions:

- *What are the benefits to inviting district human resources staff to campus for discussing personnel matters with the full administration team?*
- *Why is it important to involve all administrators when planning for staffing?*
- *How does jointly planning for faculty recruiting benefit both the school and the district?*

All of the school's administrators were gathered in the conference room by the time the director of human resources (HR) arrived to meet with them. Pleasantries were exchanged, complete with inquiries about the recent winter holidays. Sitting down to business, the HR director reviewed anticipated enrollment numbers for the next school year. The AP in charge of registration discussed the formula with her and confirmed the numbers were accurate. Translating that figure into personnel needs, the director presented the number of teachers that could be funded for the upcoming year. All parties reviewed the openings that would be created by increased student enrollment, and shared information regarding existing teachers who might transfer or resign at the end of the year. The principal and AP of instruction discussed instructional leadership needs that could develop as a result of potential changes. Together, school and district administrators developed a recruitment strategy to maximize the quality of applicants to fill the school's upcoming needs.

Figure 5.4. Analysis Table 16

Directions: For each of the preceding scenarios, circle the level of trust between the school and the community with an "L" (low), "M" (medium), or "H" (high) in the appropriate column. If helpful, note any evidence for your rating. Repeat this process to rate the level of preparation of the staff to interact with the community and the overall outcome of the situation. Finally, make note of any thoughts that you can apply to your own leadership in the Notes column. You should use these later to build your action plan.

	Trust between School and Community	Preparation of Staff to Interact with Community	Overall Outcome
Scenario 46	L M H Evidence:	L M H Evidence:	L M H Evidence:
Notes:			
Scenario 47	L M H Evidence:	L M H Evidence:	L M H Evidence:
Notes:			
Scenario 48	L M H Evidence:	L M H Evidence:	L M H Evidence:
Notes:			

Discussion

In a healthy organization, communication is essential to the well-being of all stakeholders. When people become mired in "keeping their jobs" rather than "doing their jobs," the flow of honest communication is lost. The organization chokes. By any measure, the opposite of servant leadership is the "power trip." This occurs when we identify ourselves through our position, rather than what we contribute. The myth of power encourages this dysfunction. The further up the hierarchy one goes, the greater the temptation is to grab at the myth. When we realize the only way to truly transform others is through serving their true needs, we can accept the humility of leadership. We know our purpose is to remove barriers of progress and develop everyone to capitalize on their potential.

Even as we work to flatten the hierarchy by sharing leadership responsibility through our organization, others might work to keep a clear pecking order. Regardless of rank, positions are created within an organization to help move along the business of the group. In other words, certain people are given certain tasks to accomplish to meet the needs of the group. When a power monger enters the picture, you might find abuses occurring to that system. Goods and services might be granted to some and not to others in exchange for specific self-serving behaviors. This encourages the disintegration of communication through open channels. The politics of the smoke-filled room become the norm, and "fair" looses its meaning.

Rather than succumb to power leadership, a servant leader seeks stabilization of the community. This stabilization is rooted in the conceptualization of the purpose of the organization. When we focus on the reason we are in business, we can align our management with that purpose. Again, listening to those involved, and empathizing with their thoughts, feelings, and needs help us to build a common awareness of the need for open communication. We must persuade others to allow the same opportunities to everyone, avoiding the use of political distribution of resources. This is not an easy thing to do. It takes strength to stand up to political dysfunction. For this reason, we must demonstrate our commitment to the growth of all our people, starting with ourselves. To heal deep-rooted injustices, more communication, understanding, empathy, and clear management are needed. Systemic changes begin with one person at a time.

Communication is crucial to strong relationships. Sharing information along the organizational hierarchy serves to flatten the hierarchy. We all become part of the same objective when we share information. We move in the same direction because we are trusted to interpret the information freely shared. We share responsibility for creating the best outcome for our organization. All members pool their knowledge and skills to solve problems and make improvements.

This shared ownership of organizational responsibility provides a security blanket to our harried educational society. A school district can retain a wide network of experts in various areas, which can be available to any particular building through efficient and open communication. Rather than arrogantly trying to hide potential issues, we can share them with those able to assist us to better serve our community. Again, we find the humility necessary in being an effective leader; we know our limitations as well as our strengths. We put the best interests of our school community before our ego and tap into the resources available to help us. When this mindset extends beyond the individual and is rampant through the organization, the supportive network of expertise is extended outside of the organization. This spreads the sphere of servant leaders' influence, benefiting ever more people. With more people sharing leadership of our organization, we pool our combined strengths and temper our shortcomings. In essence, we are better and stronger when we share leadership, regardless of position.

Self-Assessment

- What is your district's philosophy about teachers and/or staff dealing directly with the central office?
- Have you fully developed a professional relationship with the individuals, as well as the departments, of your central office?
- Are there hidden agendas within your district operations?
- Does your staff trust you to work on their best interests with the central office?
- Do the individuals of the central office trust you to make sound decisions?
- Are you sensitive to your supervisor's need to know what is happening at your school?
- Do you let the central office know what services you need to make your school most successful?
- What steps have you taken to initiate district resources to benefit all schools?
- Does your central office bureaucracy help, or hinder, the business of your school?
- How can you work with the central office to better serve the needs of your school?

Having completed the analysis charts for all topics in this chapter, focus on your Notes column for each. Use your notes to complete this action plan (Figure 5.5) for applying these ideas to your own leadership style.

Figure 5.5. Action Plan 4

Addressing Cultural Awareness

Goal: (Describe your school at its multicultural best.)

_____

_____

_____

Assessment: (How and when will you measure your progress toward your goal?)

_____

_____

_____

Action Steps:

1._____

_____

_____

2. _____

_____

_____

3. _____

_____

_____

_____

Promoting Parent Involvement

Goal: (Describe the level and manner of parental involvement you want at your school.)

_____

_____

_____

Assessment: (How and when will you measure your progress toward your goal?)

_____

_____

_____

Action Steps:

1._____

_____

_____

2._____

_____

_____

3._____

_____

_____

_____

Promoting Community Participation

Goal: (Describe the level and manner of interaction you want between your school and its community.)

_____

_____

_____

Assessment: (How and when will you measure your progress toward your goal?)

_____

_____

_____

Action Steps:

1._____

_____

_____

2._____

_____

_____

3. _____

_____

_____

_____

Working with the Central Office

Goal: (Describe the relationship and resources you want from your central office.)

_____

_____

_____

Assessment: (How and when will you measure your progress toward your goal?)

_____

_____

_____

Action Steps:

1._____

_____

_____

2. _____

_____

_____

3. _____

_____

_____

_____

6

Follow the Leader

There is no limit to the number of obstacles you will face when using a servant leader approach. Our system, although progressing in implementing modern leadership theory, is still heavily influenced by top-down management practices of the past. You will find many of your leadership peers and many of your followers are quite comfortable with that approach to leadership. "Just tell me what you want me to do and I'll do it," can be much easier, and less taxing than putting the effort into being part of collaborative growth. Indeed, there are legitimate instances when a directive approach is the appropriate style of leadership. This is why we must examine what makes it appropriate to outwardly step outside of the servant leadership style, and prepare ourselves to maintain its philosophy while doing what must be done. Otherwise, we become susceptible to the "dark side" of power, seduced by the quick and easy way of getting things done.

"Servant leader" is not synonymous with "weakling." It takes a high degree of confidence in one's leadership skills to know how to empower others to assume levels of leadership. It takes dedication to put the interests of the organization over our own. It takes personal strength to continually seek out and remove barriers to optimal performance. Indeed, the weakest form of leadership can be that which relies solely on power brokerage. At best, power wielding results in compliance with expectations. At its worst, it results in deep resentment and all the dysfunction that results from that. Notice how the following leader had to confront those who thought his commitment to collaboration meant they could wrangle control of the school's direction.

Scenario 49

Yet another faculty meeting seemed hijacked by "the trio"—three like-minded colleagues that routinely blocked any forward action in these meetings. No matter what the topic, or who proposed it, one of these three could be counted on to apply the brakes. "I'm sorry, but I need more information on that before I could ever agree to that." "I don't see how that would benefit the faculty at all." They were in rare form today, however. Instead of limiting their coordinated attacks to just the idea at hand, this time they targeted the messenger. "Bob has no more experience in budget process than any of us. I could never support a plan proposed by someone without any expertise in the area." Then, the unexpected happened. The democratically minded principal stood up and said bluntly, "Mr. Jones, you need to sit down and be quiet." A stunned silence followed the near audible gasp, as the faculty realized input had just been stifled by their leader. How long had their voices been silenced by the so-called democratic process, under the domination of the trio? Had the principal changed his mind about an open forum, or were there limits to what could be said in the name of collaboration?

Sharing leadership is not an excuse to abdicate one's leadership duties. It is not a method to avoid necessary confrontation. We cannot be lured into the trap of handling uncomfortable situations by allowing anyone to bully others. We must have the strength to confront anyone seeking to exert power rather than capitalize on collaboration and service toward others and the organization. Routine delegation of dealing with unpleasant situations does not embody the essence of servant-hood, either. Instead, it is top-down leadership and an abuse of authority on at least two levels. The first is by heaping problems onto others (rather than removing them), and the second is by using power to make others do something that is the leader's responsibility. Again, you must be strong to serve through your leadership. Examine how the principal below sabotaged any chance her new assistant principal (AP) had in making a positive impact on the school by delegating all the "dirty work" to him. Dirty work does not by itself corrupt leaders into power freaks. It is when leaders are not prepared to apply the servant philosophy to such duties that they tend to step into the "dark side" of leading.

Scenario 50

The principal did not perform well when meeting with departments because she felt their questions were veiled complaints. She interpreted this as dissatisfaction and found the process emotionally draining. She would preach her vision consistently, yet the faculty kept hammering her with questions about their departments. Her new AP seemed eager to take over meeting with the departments, so she quickly delegated that duty to him. He soon established a solid buffer between her and the staff, dealing with their issues for her. Originally, he was hired as a competent instructional leader with proven experience in leading faculty through the complicated accreditation process. His duties were to work with the curriculum committee, facilitate the accreditation process the school was facing, mediate academic problems, and develop teachers. As the principal delegated more "personnel problems" to him, he found less time to perform his original duties. He found himself putting teachers on remediation and disciplining them, and breaking bad news about budget to the departments. He found the faculty pandered to him for favors, and he liked it. The staff told him what he wanted to hear, and appeared to do what he told them to do. It was a big surprise to him, and his principal, when the accreditation process exposed a complete failure in collaboration, tanked morale, and zero improvement in student achievement.

By avoiding unpleasantness, we might feel more positive in our jobs, but it doesn't make the "nasties" go away. Left unattended, wounds fester. Ignore a festering wound and it turns gangrenous. This approach does not serve anyone's interest and should be the only thing avoided. Requiring others to carry out unpleasant tasks for us, especially when they haven't fully developed a servant leadership philosophy, is an invitation for disaster. We have addressed in previous chapters how to use staff participation to mitigate much of the unpleasant duties in administration. Having the courage to handle what is left over in a firm but caring manner is the cost of being a servant leader.

When we examine whether a servant approach is appropriate, or if a directive approach is necessary, we need to focus on the "cannot" concept. "Cannot" is not the same principle as "choose not to." "Cannot" invokes a powerlessness to do something, whereas when we "choose not to" do something, we are empowered. If something must be done for the good of the organization or to fulfill our shared vision but is not done, we need to determine why it is not done. Too often, "cannot" and "choose not to" are seen as interchangeable obstacles, and treated in the same way by the leader. This is an error in leadership, however. The difference between motivations determines how best to serve through our leadership role. Note how the department chair was unable to accomplish what was expected of him in the scenario below, while the teacher was unwilling to do so.

Scenario 51

The new teacher was fully qualified to teach high school chemistry. Perhaps, with a doctorate in chemistry, he was too qualified, as he seemed unable to teach to the appropriate level. Student and parent complaints continued to pour into the principal's office. Correction of the situation was delegated to the department chair, although authority in the matter was not. Confident in his superior credentials, the teacher scoffed at the chair's suggestions. Without administrative backing, the chair had no legitimate power to make the teacher change his methods. The chair's requests for administrative action were ignored, and the teacher's performance evaluations met expectations. The department chair, however, found a "needs improvement" on his chair evaluation under "ability to lead instruction of department members."

It is unethical to punish an individual for failing to achieve that which we (as leaders) have blocked them from achieving. We must enable those around us, especially those reliant on us, to accomplish what we expect from them. This requires giving them what is needed to do so, including resources, training, and motivation. If our follower is unable to do what must be done, we need to provide appropriate instruction and ensure other obstacles preventing success are removed. However, when the follower is *able* to do what is required, but *elects* not to do it, we need to take a different approach.

Scenario 52

Although she was new to the school, the principal made a point to know all of the faculty and staff by name by the start of the school year. Surprisingly, she discovered that she was the only one who did, as members of the staff had operated in isolation over their years at the school. Determined to develop a team feeling within the school, the principal organized a phone festival during the first week of school. Teachers were asked to make "welcome" calls to all of their parents. Pizza and soda was purchased as an incentive to draw faculty into a common phone room to help develop camaraderie. Only nine teachers and one counselor showed up to make their calls within the team atmosphere. Others actually came by to collect their pizza and return to their classrooms to make their calls in private.

In this case, we need to explore the motivation behind the followers' choices before selecting the appropriate correction to implement. All obstacles to making phone calls in a common area were addressed. Phones were available for each teacher, as were chairs and desk space. Promotion of the event was made with enthusiasm. The majority of the teachers simply chose not to participate in this team-building activity. Applying instruction in team behavior would likely be a waste of time and effort and would possibly be scoffed at in this case. A more covert application of "service" becomes necessary to provide the leadership action, in whatever form necessary, to motivate each follower to participate.

Service behavior can be learned, and the outcomes are worth our efforts. We lead to serve others, serve the organization, serve society, and serve ourselves, too. To do this, we change the "power" attitude inherent in leadership positions. We replace "power of leadership" with "service of leadership" in our philosophies and our actions. With consistent practice, any threats we perceive to our leadership will be overcome through our service to the organization. We make ourselves indispensable to the spirit and operation of the organization, even if it is by empowering others to take the action. Not all people accept a servant leader easily. Those with little trust in others will find it easier to change their perception of reality to fit their beliefs than to change their beliefs to fit reality. The delusions of these few should not deter us from leading through service. The truth is: Leading shouldn't make us suffer. When we are committed to serving others through our leadership, every trial is a gift.

When we are servant leaders, we are not always out in front of the pack. Sometimes, we operate from inside the pack to allow others to lead in areas of their expertise. The top dog is not always the strongest, loudest, most aggressive member; it is the one with the most confidence, the most personal control, and the most relaxed about moving the pack forward. Even without the spotlight on us, our leadership is evident in the way we ensure success of both co-leaders and followers by identifying and removing obstacles. As mentioned before, when hiking, sometimes leaders bring followers along quicker if they step aside to hold a branch back from whacking others. This is the art of leadership that stems from common sense, which is not as common as it needs to be. Making servant-hood our daily stance programs our actions in such a way that common sense prevails in our everyday behavior. Servant leadership is a philosophy, a way of life, not a hard-and-fast model. Live it, breathe it, be it.

Figure 6.1. Progress Assessment Plan 1

Review each chapter's Action Plan. Copy the goals you made into this chart (Figure 6.1), along with when and how you will assess your progress on each. As you complete your assessments, note your progress in the column provided. Determine what further action steps are needed to meet each goal. Adjust your goals, if necessary, based on continual self-assessment of your servant leadership behaviors.

Goal	Assessment	Date Due	Progress	Next Steps

Goal	Assessment	Date Due	Progress	Next Steps

Goal	Assessment	Date Due	Progress	Next Steps

Goal	Assessment	Date Due	Progress	Next Steps

References

American Heritage Dictionary of the English Language, 4th Ed. (2000). Boston: Houghton Mifflin.

Collins, J. C. (2001). *Good to Great: Why Some Companies Make the Leap...and Others Don't.* New York: Harper Collins.

Covey, S. R. (1994). Merrill, A. R., & Merrill, R. R. (1996). *First Things First.* New York: Simon & Shuster.

De Pree, M. (1989). *Leadership Is an Art.* New York: Bantam Doubleday.

Greenleaf, R. K. (1970). *The Servant as Leader.* Indianapolis, IN: The Robert Greeleaf Center.

Greenleaf, R. K. (1991). *The Servant as Leader.* Indianapolis, IN: The Robert Greeleaf Center.

Greenleaf, R. K. (1991). *The Servant-Leader Within: A Transformative Path.* Beazley, H., Beggs, J., & Spears, L. C. (Eds). New York: Paulist Press.